UNC | SCHOOL OF GOVERNMENT

The Law of Municipal Streets and Utility Easements in North Carolina

CHARLES SZYPSZAK

The School of Government at the University of North Carolina at Chapel Hill works to improve the lives of North Carolinians by engaging in practical scholarship that helps public officials and citizens understand and improve state and local government. Established in 1931 as the Institute of Government, the School provides educational, advisory, and research services for state and local governments. The School of Government is also home to a nationally ranked Master of Public Administration program, the North Carolina Judicial College, and specialized centers focused on community and economic development, information technology, and environmental finance.

As the largest university-based local government training, advisory, and research organization in the United States, the School of Government offers up to 200 courses, webinars, and specialized conferences for more than 12,000 public officials each year. In addition, faculty members annually publish approximately 50 books, manuals, reports, articles, bulletins, and other print and online content related to state and local government. The School also produces the *Daily Bulletin Online* each day the General Assembly is in session, reporting on activities for members of the legislature and others who need to follow the course of legislation.

Operating support for the School of Government's programs and activities comes from many sources, including state appropriations, local government membership dues, private contributions, publication sales, course fees, and service contracts.

Visit sog.unc.edu or call 919.966.5381 for more information on the School's courses, publications, programs, and services.

Michael R. Smith, Dean
Thomas H. Thornburg, Senior Associate Dean
Jen Willis, Associate Dean for Development
Michael Vollmer, Associate Dean for Administration

FACULTY

Whitney Afonso
Trey Allen
Gregory S. Allison
David N. Ammons
Ann M. Anderson
Maureen Berner
Frayda S. Bluestein
Mark F. Botts
Anita R. Brown-Graham
Peg Carlson
Leisha DeHart-Davis
Shea Riggsbee Denning
Sara DePasquale
Jacquelyn Greene
Norma Houston

Cheryl Daniels Howell
Jeffrey A. Hughes
Willow S. Jacobson
Robert P. Joyce
Diane M. Juffras
Dona G. Lewandowski
Adam Lovelady
James M. Markham
Christopher B. McLaughlin
Kara A. Millonzi
Jill D. Moore
Jonathan Q. Morgan
Ricardo S. Morse
C. Tyler Mulligan
Kimberly L. Nelson

David W. Owens
William C. Rivenbark
Dale J. Roenigk
John Rubin
Jessica Smith
Meredith Smith
Carl W. Stenberg III
John B. Stephens
Charles Szypszak
Shannon H. Tufts
Aimee N. Wall
Jeffrey B. Welty
Richard B. Whisnant

Printed in the United States of America

23 22 21 20 19   1 2 3 4 5

ISBN 978-1-56011-952-4

Contents

Preface

This book is in part a sequel to Distinguished Professor David Lawrence's influential 1985 book, *Property Interests in North Carolina City Streets*, with an update and expansion on statutory and common law affecting North Carolina municipal streets and utility rights of way. Attorney Brett Berne contributed valuable research while he was completing an MPA at the School of Government.

Charles Szypszak
Albert Coates Distinguished Professor of Public Law and Government
Chapel Hill, June 2019

Dedication

This book is dedicated to those who act with integrity and a sense of personal responsibility, whether in the name of the public's interest or in the enjoyment of property rights.

Introduction

Maintaining streets and utility rights of way is among the most elemental of local government services. Routes for public travel have always connected individuals to their communities. Modern networks for water, sewer, and communications could not have developed or continue to exist without pathways across private lands. Despite the importance of enforceable rights of way to our communities, the legal source of their origins, and of the public's rights to use them, are often murky. Many rights of way became public merely with the passage of time and use, rather than with the documentary formality we normally associate with real estate acquisitions. The enforceability of these rights, and the nature of responsibilities that go along with them, depend on more than a century of case law that can be challenging to understand and, at times, difficult to reconcile.

The modern reality is that streets and utilities—and the laws governing them—are interconnected at all three levels of government—local, state, and federal—and with private development. The system is a complex array of facilities and responsibilities. The Federal Highway Administration maintains the interstate highways and other federal highways. The North Carolina Department of Transportation maintains state highways and streets outside of municipalities. Inside municipalities, the state maintains major highways and some other roads, and municipalities maintain the other non-federal public roads within their boundaries. The state and its municipalities work together to determine whether a particular public road is to be state or municipally maintained. Within this web, private development occurs, resulting in new connectors that merge into the municipal street system and beyond. This is an important part of the challenge for municipalities: being an integrated part of a national network using the limited resources available to local governments.

There are some identifiable differences within the local, state, and federal road system. Municipalities name their own roads. Counties do not maintain roads in North Carolina. North Carolina state highways include primary highways numbered under 1,000. State highways numbered higher than 1,000 are considered secondary. Federal highways are marked according to a national numbering system. Interstate routes are designed with an "I" on a red, white, and blue sign and on other federal highways with a "U.S." on a white shield. Generally, north-south interstate highways have odd numbers and east-west interstate highways have even numbers. Usually a highway has only two digits (such as I-40 or I-95); three digits are used when a highway splits around cities, with the last two digits being the same (such as I-280 and I-480). Despite these differences in naming conventions, a typical driver may not be aware of the transition from municipal to state or federal roads.

Most of the legal issues that arise concerning rights of way concern the source of public rights to roads that cross what used to be private land. Municipalities can acquire rights to private land by the same methods as any other owner: by buying it. Additionally, the government can acquire land by accepting an offer of dedication from a developer, which has become the most common method for acquisition of municipal roads. Often, disputes involving streets result from the lack of clear evidence of a completed offer of dedication and acceptance and from resolution of this ambiguity with the application of often confusing legal principles.

Disputes also arise about the interrelationship of the public's use of a street, the government's maintenance of it, and abutters' rights. The lay of the land with respect to use and maintenance is not always readily apparent. A public road that has been in use probably will have an obvious travel path, usually paved. However, the land subject to public rights usually is wider than the paved portion. Roadway widths vary, but as a typical example, two lanes of a road may be twenty-four feet wide, but the right of way may be thirty or forty feet wide. A four-lane road may be forty-eight feet wide and the right of way sixty feet wide. The additional space may be kept clear from construction or used for drainage, signs, utilities, and a sidewalk. Municipalities have the discretion to lay out these features and maintain control over them, and they have a duty to keep roads free from unnecessary obstructions and in proper repair. Still, owners along the road may have trees and landscaping, as well as such things as mailboxes, outside the paved area but within the right of way, to the extent they do not interfere with travel. The owner's ability to make improvements to this area, such as to install a driveway, is further subject to the government's regulatory powers. Local regulations also may require landowners to keep the area within the right of way in a safe condition, including trimming trees and removing obstructions to sight lines and public travel.

The law also recognizes that continued use of public streets is interconnected with private land use and development, and it therefore restricts the circumstances and procedures for closing a street. The most likely scenario in which a discontinuance occurs is when there is no foreseeable need to maintain a section of a street because development has changed. To close a street, a municipality must strictly follow a statutory procedure that aims to protect the rights of those who might still need access. Abandonment of utility easements usually does not implicate the same public concerns. Normally such an easement is not abandoned unless the municipality already has acquired alternative routes for a changed system.

Nonetheless, cities can find themselves devoting a lot of attention to defining the precise nature of uses to which easements can be put.

Such is the overview. The following chapters address the main legal questions that arise in North Carolina concerning rights of way for municipal streets and utilities, an area of the law in which the answers are not always intuitive or even clear. Real property law is mostly common law that has changed little over centuries, and the cases that still control may be written in contextual language. This book strives to summarize and, as much as possible, to synthesize this body of law governing municipalities that manage streets and utilities. I hope it will be useful to those trying to arrive at the best answers.

1

Acquisition by Conveyance

The most straightforward way for a municipality to acquire necessary rights in land for a public street or utility line is the same way by which most individuals become owners of real estate: with a voluntary conveyance in writing using the customary form of deed. Such a transaction does not involve legal vagaries that can arise with rights of way acquired through offers of dedication, which are more common than conveyances, nor does this type of arrangement involve the potential for dispute and litigation costs involved with acquiring property through an eminent domain proceeding. Nonetheless, to minimize the potential for problems, an acquisition by conveyance should be carried out with the usual expert attention to real estate transfers, as well as special considerations for municipal transactions.

1.1 Discretion to Acquire

By statute, a North Carolina municipality is authorized to "acquire and hold any property, real and personal, devised, sold, or in any manner conveyed, dedicated to, or otherwise acquired" by it.[1] For streets and utilities, municipalities customarily acquire perpetual easements, which give them the right to install, maintain, and reconfigure public improvements within the easement area according to the conditions of the acquisition. However, municipalities also have the discretion to acquire full rights to property, known as a "fee" interest.

Municipalities have discretion to determine the particular property to be acquired, provided *the use* to which it will be applied is legislatively authorized and constitutionally permissible. Decisions about public project needs are not subject to judicial scrutiny except when there are facts indicating that officials are acting in bad faith or oppressively, or when there is a manifest abuse of discretion. A municipality could not constitutionally use public funds to acquire property for a private party's exclusive use.[2] When acquiring land for a right of way, the use to which it will be put must have some public purpose or benefit, although it may

---

1. Chapter 160A, Section 11 of the North Carolina General Statutes (hereinafter G.S.).
2. State Highway Comm'n v. Batts, 265 N.C. 346, 360, 144 S.E.2d 126, 136 (1965).

be of particular use to individual landowners. As the North Carolina Supreme Court said, "The public nature of the project cannot be made to depend on a numerical count of those to be served or the smallness or largeness of a community."[3] Accordingly, an acquisition for a street extension to particular property is a public purpose as long as it is at least "an incidental part of a comprehensive and complex highway project."[4]

The courts consistently recognize that governments must be afforded wide discretion to make decisions about property to be acquired to implement public projects. As the North Carolina Supreme Court said,

> [T]he economic feasibility of the proposed use is for the legislative or administrative body to determine. With that determination the courts may not interfere, except upon a clear showing of abuse of discretion such as to make the taking of the property an arbitrary and capricious interference with the right of the owner thereto. Thus, in the absence of a showing of bad faith, . . . the courts will not interfere with the legislative or administrative determination that the taking of the particular property is necessary for the successful operation of the proposed project or prevent the taking on the ground that another site would be better, cheaper or otherwise preferable.[5]

North Carolina's courts presume that public officials have acted in good faith and according to applicable laws and regulations.[6] As long as a municipality is acquiring property for "a public purpose, courts will only intervene if the party challenging the decision can show 'bad faith, malice, wantonness, or oppressive and manifest abuse of discretion.'"[7] To fail this test, a decision must be "so arbitrary and unreasonable as to indicate malicious or wanton disregard of the rights of persons affected."[8] In a modern context, the most likely scenario in which good faith might be questionable is when a municipal official has a financial interest in the acquisition, as might be the case if the official owns the property being acquired or property that will become more valuable because of the acquisition.

---

3. City of Charlotte v. Heath, 226 N.C. 750, 755, 40 S.E.2d 600, 604 (1946).

4. N.C. State Highway Comm'n v. Asheville Sch., Inc., 276 N.C. 556, 562, 173 S.E.2d 909, 914 (1970).

5. Vance Cty. v. Royster, 271 N.C. 53, 60, 155 S.E.2d 790, 795 (1967) (citations omitted).

6. Bd. of Ed. of Hickory Admin. Sch. Unit v. Seagle, 120 N.C. App. 566, 571, 463 S.E.2d 277, 281 (1995).

7. City of Monroe v. W.F. Harris Dev., LLC, 131 N.C. App. 22, 24–25, 505 S.E.2d 160, 162 (1998) (quoting Greensboro-Highpoint Airport Auth. v. Irvin, 36 N.C. App. 662, 665, 245 S.E.2d 390, 392 (1978)).

8. Newton v. Sch. Comm. of Charlotte, 158 N.C. 186, 188, 73 S.E. 886, 887 (1912).

As the North Carolina Supreme Court said, "The courts are astute to impeach and invalidate any transaction where an official has any personal interest whatever in the matter decided by him."[9] This does not mean that a municipality cannot acquire property under such circumstances. Merely owning property near a proposed right of way is not sufficient to impugn an official's motives.[10]

To avoid questions about intent, an official who stands to gain personally from a property conveyance probably should not participate in making the purchase decision, and the personal interest should be fully disclosed. A state statute specifically restricts personally benefitted local officials from being involved in committing a municipality to a contract to purchase real estate.[11] Someone who will directly benefit from a contract may not be involved in making the contract or administering it, nor may the person attempt to influence those who will.[12] The statutory restriction does not only apply to someone who benefits directly. An individual is deemed to benefit impermissibly if the individual or the individual's spouse has more than a 10 percent interest in an entity that is a party to the acquisition contract or derives any income or commission from it.[13] The restrictions apply to anyone who is elected or appointed to act on behalf of the municipality, as well as to any public official or employee who would oversee contract performance or have authority to make decisions about the contract or to interpret it.[14] Prohibited involvement includes participating in developing the contract's terms or specifications.[15] The statutory contract prohibitions do not prevent a municipality from acquiring property from a municipal officer or employee and paying that individual just compensation, by means of an eminent domain proceeding, as described in section 4.1, *infra*.[16] Completing the judicial process in such a proceeding settles any challenge that the municipality is acquiring the property improperly or for something other than the constitutionally required compensation.

Although a municipality has discretion to choose what to acquire, certain acquisitions can affect private property in ways that could entitle owners to compensation. This may occur, for example, if the land being acquired is subject to restrictive covenants and the public use will violate those covenants in a way that diminishes the value of land that benefits from them. In *City of Raleigh v. Edwards,*[17]

---

9. Venable v. Sch. Comm. of Pilot Mountain, 149 N.C. 120, 122, 62 S.E., 902, 903 (1908).

10. Kistler v. Bd. of Educ., 233 N.C. 400, 406, 64 S.E.2d 403, 407 (1951).

11. G.S. 14-234.

12. G.S. 14-234(a).

13. G.S. 14-234(a1)(4).

14. G.S. 14-234(a1).

15. G.S. 14-234(a1)(3).

16. G.S. 14-234(b)(2).

17. 235 N.C. 671, 71 S.E.2d 396 (1952).

landowners challenged the city's power to take property for an elevated water storage tank in a subdivision that limited uses to dwellings. The North Carolina Supreme Court noted that the subdivision's landowners could not enforce the restrictions against the municipality, which could have overriden them with its power of eminent domain.[18] However, the court also instructed that the municipality's violation of the covenants was a taking of the other owners' property rights and entitled them to compensation "commensurate with any loss they may sustain."[19]

A municipality could also be required to pay compensation if it acquires property under certain conditions but later violates them. For example, in *Bessemer Improvement Co. v. City of Greensboro*,[20] a municipality agreed to take over private streets and the owner of the property on which the streets were located agreed to pay into a maintenance fund while reserving the right to cross the streets with railroad tracks. The municipality's plans changed, and it conveyed the land to the state for a limited-access highway that would not allow the defendant owner's tracks. The court said that the municipality had the right to opt out of the commitment, "but this does not relieve it of the obligation of paying the fair and just value of the property rights which it acquired by virtue of its unenforceable promise."[21]

A municipality's reasonable discretion to acquire land for public streets and utilities also extends to the amount it pays to the seller. A real property parcel is considered unique, and no statutorily required competitive bidding procedures are implicated when a municipality acquires real property for a public purpose. Unless an abuse of discretion can be shown—or a specific constitutional or statutory provision is violated—a court will not invalidate an acquisition because of the consideration paid.[22] The price therefore need not be matched to tax assessment or market value. To challenge a price, a party would have to prove that the municipality's decision makers "acted in wanton disregard of public good."[23] Courts have sustained payments of two and two-and-one-half times the alleged "reasonable value" as squarely within the municipality's discretion.[24] Relevant factors in considering the reasonableness of a price include the uncertainty and volatility of market-based valuations and the avoidance of costs that otherwise would be incurred if the municipality had to take the property with eminent domain proceedings.

---

18. *Id.* at 677, 71 S.E.2d at 401.

19. *Id.* at 679, 71 S.E.2d at 402.

20. 247 N.C. 549, 101 S.E.2d 336 (1958).

21. *Id.* at 553, 101 S.E.2d at 340.

22. Painter v. Wake Cty. Bd. of Educ., 288 N.C. 165, 217 S.E.2d 650 (1975).

23. *Id.* at 179, 217 S.E.2d at 659 (quoting Barbour v. Carteret Cty., 255 N.C. 177, 181, 120 S.E.2d 448, 451 (1961)).

24. *Id.* at 178–79, 217 S.E.2d at 659.

A contract that requires payment of money by a municipality must be certified as pre-audited by the government unit's finance officer or by a deputy finance officer whom the unit's council has authorized.[25] This pre-audit requirement confirms that the funds for the purchase are in the municipality's budget. By statute, this certificate must take substantially the following form: "This instrument has been preaudited in the manner required by the Local Government Budget and Fiscal Control Act."[26]

Municipalities may enter into purchase arrangements in which they grant a security interest, such as with a deed of trust given in connection with a mortgage loan, to the seller or lender who is "advancing moneys or supplying financing for the purchase transaction" of an interest in real property, provided the municipality holds a public hearing of which ten days' prior published notice must be given.[27] However, a state statute imposes requirements on the structure of installment financing. The local government must take title to the property—installment contracts with transfer of title after payment is complete are not permitted. Prior approval from the Local Government Commission (LGC) is required for loans with certain terms or amounts, as specified by statute.[28] A state statute prohibits any deficiency judgments against local governments.[29] A municipality may not pledge its taxing power to secure payments due under real property purchase arrangements.[30] Without a special act, a municipality may not accept property as payment of taxes.[31]

1.2 Authorized Officials

By statute, a municipality's governing council has the power to act in behalf of the municipality in property acquisitions.[32] The municipality's charter could have restrictions on, or special procedures for, the way in which that power is exercised.[33] Either the charter or the council may delegate authority to the mayor in a

---

25. G.S. 159-28(a1).

26. *Id.*

27. G.S. 160A-20(a), (g).

28. G.S. 159-149. The LGC, created by the North Carolina General Assembly in 1931, "provides assistance to local governments and public authorities in North Carolina" in the areas of borrowing, selling debt, oversight, and auditing. *See* N.C. Dep't of State Treasurer, *About the Local Government Commission*, NCTREASURER.COM, https://www.nctreasurer.com/slg/Pages/Local-Government-Commission.aspx.

29. G.S. 160A-20(f).

30. *Id.*

31. G.S. 105-357(a). For an example of such a special act, see S.L. 1985-910 (City of Wilmington, Town of Farmville, City of Salisbury, and Durham County).

32. G.S. 160A-12, -66, -67.

33. G.S. 160A-3.

municipality with a council-mayor form of government,[34] or to the manager in a council-manager municipality.[35] A duly-approved council resolution authorizing the mayor or manager to sign instruments for a real property purchase transaction should satisfy a seller and title examiner about the signatory's authority.

The state's public meetings statutes enable the council to meet in closed session to establish or give instructions about price and other material terms of a potential contract for the acquisition of real property.[36] This authority only applies if the property is to be acquired "by purchase, option, exchange, or lease,"[37] which does not include receipt of donated property. The council also may meet in closed session to consult with an attorney about bringing, handling, or settling an eminent domain action to acquire property.[38]

Before entering into an agreement with a municipality, legal counsel for the seller of real property will likely want to ensure that the municipality's representative has due authority to enter into an agreement. Anyone dealing with the municipality has good reason to want to confirm a particular official's authority to enter into and consummate an agreement. As the North Carolina Court of Appeals explained, "'[P]ersons dealing with a municipal corporation are charged with notice of all limitations upon the authority of its officers representing them.'"[39] "This is because the scope of such authority is a matter of public record."[40] When a contract is void for lack of authority or noncompliance with a statutory prerequisite, a party may not recover damages from reliance on the void agreement.[41] Although contracts routinely recite that an officer is "duly authorized," problems can arise if the officer acted without getting requisite approvals from the governing body. To guard against this possibility, the party's legal counsel will check the municipality's organizational documents and, if any approvals are required, structure the arrangement so that they are obtained in due course. The council also should consider being clear about who has authority to sign in its behalf, to avoid complications for itself or for parties with which it is dealing.

---

34. G.S. 160A-66.

35. G.S. 160A-148(8).

36. G.S. 143-318.11(a)(5).

37. *Id.*

38. G.S. 143-318.11(a)(3).

39. Moody v. Transylvania Cty., 271 N.C. 384, 389, 156 S.E.2d 716, 720 (1967) (quoting 38 Aм. Jur. *Municipal Corporations* § 522, at 202).

40. L & S Leasing, Inc. v. City of Winston-Salem, 122 N.C. App. 619, 622, 471 S.E.2d 118, 120 (1996).

41. Data Gen. Corp. v. Cty. of Durham, 143 N.C. App. 97, 103–04, 545 S.E.2d 243, 248 (2001).

1.3 Deeds

Despite the seeming regularity of deeds, each is in some ways unique, and the effect of a deed's details on property interests can turn on subtle and sometimes surprising common law rules. A deed is an expression of a grantor's intent, later to be interpreted and enforced by strangers who examine it in the public record. A well-drafted deed precisely and fully describes the particular rights, title, and interests pertaining to real property, using language that will be unambiguously understood within the transactional community. This brief discussion about deeds is intended to give a sense of the basics and is no substitute for the advice of a knowledgeable real estate attorney.

A municipality should be careful to ensure that any deed conveying property to it for a right of way contains all the necessary elements, clearly stated in detail that conform to sound real estate conveyance practice. In North Carolina's real property recording system, parties bear full responsibility for making proper recordings. Registers of deeds do not review instruments presented to them to determine if they are legally valid. Nor do registers check or confirm that an instrument creates enforceable ownership rights. Registers only review presented instruments to see if they meet format requirements, which are discussed in greater detail in the text below.

One required component for a deed to be valid that receives particularly careful attention is the presence of a notary's seal or other official acknowledgment (this requirement also applies to instruments such as easement agreements, deeds of trust, and powers of attorney). Deeds that require but do not have such an acknowledgment may be subject to challenge as invalid to convey the property. The North Carolina Supreme Court has held that a real estate instrument is denied the benefits of the recording statute if it lacks a required component of a proper registration with the register of deeds.[42] This rule is reason for paying very careful attention to the drafting and recording of deeds. Someone who notices an invalidating defect could acquire a competing interest and claim priority of rights in the subject property because the previously recorded instrument should be denied registration status.

There is no requirement that the contents of a deed state how much is being paid for the property. However, someone who presents a deed must report the amount of excise tax that is due, which is based on the consideration paid for the property. A statewide excise tax equal to $1 per $500 of payment is due on most deeds, including deeds to municipalities. An exemption from the excise tax applies to a government entity when it sells and receives payment, not when the entity is

---

42. McClure v. Crow, 196 N.C. 657, 659–60, 146 S.E. 713, 714–15 (1929).

a buyer that is making payments.[43] By North Carolina special acts, an additional county excise tax of $1 per $100 of consideration applies in several eastern counties.[44] Consequently, the price that the seller reports as being paid for property can be seen on the public record based on the stamp showing the excise tax paid. Language within a deed such as "for $10 and other good consideration" is a traditional formality to show that something was paid for the property; it is not seen as indicating what was actually paid.

To be recordable with the register of deeds, a deed must meet other format and informational requirements, including payment of recording fees. Municipalities are not exempt from paying register of deeds recording fees. On its first page, a deed or deed of trust must show the name of its drafter.[45] By resolution, county commissioners may impose certain additional requirements allowed by statute. For instance, they may require that real-property-purchase-related instruments show the new owner's permanent mailing address and the name and address of the person to whom the instrument is to be returned.[46] If a county uses parcel identifier numbers (PINs), it may require them to be shown on the instrument and verified by the county before a deed can be recorded.[47] Counties also have various requirements for certifications that property taxes have been paid or will be paid from closing proceeds, which are governed by state acts and county resolutions authorized by those acts. Each county should be checked for its specific requirements.

Registers do not check the contents of deeds or give advice about them. The parties to the real property arrangement decide what they want to convey and how to describe it. A "warranty deed" is the most common instrument used for this purpose. With this warranty, a grantor promises fully to transfer lawful possession free of others' rights except as disclosed in the deed and free of deeds of trust or other liens except as stated in the deed, and also promises to defend the title against claims that breach the warranty. Warranty deeds are the norm in residential transactions, especially when the buyer is obtaining secured financing, because buyers and lenders are expecting the maximum assurances about title. With conveyances to municipalities, buyers often give deeds with more confined assurances. A grantor giving "special warranty" covenants promises to defend the grantee only against claims involving any prior transfers by the grantor, including prior conveyances of the premises, deeds of trust, easements, or other rights in

---

43. G.S. 105-228.28.
44. 1985 N.C. Sess. Laws ch. 954 (Camden); 1985 N.C. Sess. Laws ch. 881 (Chowan); 1985 N.C. Sess. Laws ch. 670 (Currituck); 1985 N.C. Sess. Laws ch. 525 (Dare); 1989 N.C. Sess. Laws ch. 393 (Pasquotank, Perquimans, Washington).
45. G.S. 47-17.1.
46. G.S. 161-30(a).
47. G.S. 161-30(b).

the land. In North Carolina, a conveyance of property by "quitclaim" is "as is." It is normally used in circumstances in which the title to the property is unclear or in dispute, or as part of a settlement, such as upon a divorce. This form of deed is sometimes called a "non-warranty" or "no-warranty" deed.

A municipality acquiring property by deed will want to be clear about the property's boundaries, which usually requires reliance upon a survey, either one already in existence or one engaged specifically for the project. Though most deeds are drafted according to what is customary, the parties to the property transfer decide how they are going to describe what it is that is being transferred. The most common approach is to include a reference to a recorded plat and a metes and bounds property description, with recitation of distances and compass headings. If something is omitted, or if the description is so problematic that the parties' intent cannot be determined, disputes can arise. A municipality should carefully study the property description in any deed to which it is a party, compare it to how markers and other signs of boundaries appear on the ground, and ask for further clarification whenever the two do not clearly match.

A grantee must accept a deed for it to be effective to convey the described property.[48] A landowner cannot unilaterally convey property or an interest in it without the grantee's explicit or implied acceptance. Accordingly, a landowner cannot give an easement for a street merely by executing and recording a deed—no conveyance occurs unless the municipality accepts the deed in some fashion.

1.4 Record Title

A municipal real property acquisition can become complicated and costly if the municipality relies on a deed without ensuring that the owner who gives it has the power to do so free of others' rights. Landowners can only convey what they own.

North Carolina is one of the very few states with a "pure" race version of statutory scheme governing the priority of competing claims to the same property. The North Carolina statutes provide that no deed or other instrument of conveyance "shall be valid to pass any property interest as against lien creditors or purchasers for a valuable consideration from the donor, bargainor or lessor but from the time of registration thereof in the county where the land lies."[49] Once properly recorded, a deed gives what is known as "constructive notice" to anyone who might later be

---

48. Messer v. Laurel Hill Assocs., 93 N.C. App. 439, 445, 378 S.E.2d 220, 224 (1989).
49. G.S. 47-18(a); *see also id.* § 47-27 (requiring recording of easement deeds).

interested in the property. This means that everyone is deemed to know about a recorded document regardless of whether it is actually seen at the register of deeds.

To determine rights to real estate based on the recorded instruments, a title searcher looks for a "chain of title" of conveyances over time. In North Carolina, instruments are recorded in the order in which they are presented, and they can be found within the register's index of the names of the parties to the instruments. In a typical search, the searcher will begin with the current owner's name and the recording information for the owner's deed, then work backward using the name index for a search period. The search period typically goes back about thirty years, a duration usually considered sufficiently long to detect problems for practical purposes. Instruments will be checked for possible adverse claims. A title searcher will look at other public records as well, such as tax records and court files. Assessment of the state of title requires the expertise of a real estate attorney.

One of the most common interests for which title examiners search is enforceable security interests such as deeds of trust given by prior owners. A title examiner will search back in time to ensure that there are records of satisfaction for all deeds of trust that once applied to the property. Recorded security interests are protected property rights, and a municipality has the same concern about them as does any other buyer. Other common title concerns for which examiners search are easements, covenants, and other rights that the owner has not disclosed. As with security interests, these encumbrances are not automatically extinguished upon a conveyance.

Individuals commonly misperceive tax listings to be the title record. Tax listings are based on tentative ownership information as shown on certain public records, as well as on statutory presumptions. The listings are not a determination of actual title. They can, however, be relevant information in property disputes. For instance, payment of taxes can be a factor in resolving disputes about whether a street has been established through years of adverse use, because it is some evidence about whether an owner is aware of a public claim.[50] Additionally, paying taxes on property with clearly marked boundaries shown on a recorded survey can shorten the length of time someone must occupy that property before claiming it based on occupancy.[51] However, the tax listing is only a starting point for investigating title, and a full assessment requires expert examination of the recorded chain of instruments and other public records and facts.

As noted earlier, this chapter is only a summary of typical real estate instruments and the real estate transactional process in general. Rights to real estate, including for public streets and easements, may turn on perplexing property law

---

50. Dep't of Transp. v. Haggerty, 127 N.C. App. 499, 502, 492 S.E.2d 770, 772 (1997).
51. G.S. 1-38.

principles, subtleties in the way instruments are drafted, and facts that would not seem important until there is a dispute. For example, one special consideration that applies to governments in their acquisition of real property is that ownership is sometimes for a particular, exclusive public purpose—such as for a public building—and sometimes for open public actual use—such as for a street. Problems can arise when the parties involved are unclear about which purpose is intended. An illustration of this potential arose in *Smith v. County of Durham*,[52] where an easement that property owners said was intended for access to a single privately owned lot was later deemed to be for public use after a local government took title to the benefitted lot. On a plat prepared for getting regulatory approval for a home lot, the landowners showed an easement to enable an abutter to connect to a public street. Several years later, the county acquired the abutting tract to implement an open space plan. The deed to the county referred to the easement without any reference to it being a public road and expressly disclaimed any warranty in connection with the easement.[53] Nevertheless, the North Carolina Court of Appeals held that depiction of the easement on the plat was an "express dedication of an easement for the use and benefit of the public, including" the county.[54] The court noted that the owners signed a certificate on the plat showing that "all public and private streets, easements, and other areas so designated upon said plat are hereby dedicated for such use."[55] However, the easement at issue was shown on that plat as an access easement with no indication of public travel.[56] The outcome of *Smith v. County of Durham* illustrates the importance of being very clear about an easement's intended location and scope, and it is a reminder that the consequences of imprecision can be unpredictable.

---

52. 214 N.C. App. 423, 714 S.E.2d 849 (2011).
53. Deed recorded at Book 5933, Page 608 of the Durham County Registry of Deeds.
54. 214 N.C. App. at 435, 714 S.E.2d at 857.
55. *Id.*
56. *Id.* at 430–31, 714 S.E.2d at 854.

2

Acquisition by Offer of Dedication and Acceptance

Public rights to a street often cannot be tied to a recorded deed conveying the land across which the street runs, or an easement in it, to a municipality. Traditionally, a right of way became public when a developer set aside a strip of land to connect subdivided lots to the road system, and a municipality added the right of way to its maintenance network. In today's highly-regulated development environment, dedication and acceptance of a street probably will be documented on recorded subdivision plats that received local regulatory approval. Much of the law governing dedication and acceptance emerged when such documentation was not as carefully managed and there was less clear evidence of the developer's and municipality's intent.

One reason why dedication and acceptance may be preferred to acquisition by other means is that with proper management of the process, the municipality can take responsibility for the street only after the developer improves it to meet municipal design specifications for such things as base and surface, width and gradients, and curbing. On the other hand, acquisition by conveyance or eminent domain may be more appropriate if the municipality wants control over the layout as part of a long-range plan that involves more than a simple public street, as may be the case if other public infrastructure is anticipated.

The law of street dedication is mostly common law, stemming from cases in which there was a dispute about the existence of a public street. The cases tend to fall into two main categories. In some cases, a municipality insisted that it had the power to maintain a street without having a clearly documented source of its acquisition, and a landowner argued that the rights either never existed or were lost. In others, those who wanted use of a public right of way insisted that it had been acquired over someone's land through the passage of time. Courts have been inclined to uphold public rights to a road over which the government has exercised control, in large part because, historically, public streets were welcomed without need for formal procedures. A new public road meant better connections and higher real estate values. When users claimed public access over the land of another that was never maintained by the municipality, the courts have tended to be protective of private ownership and unwilling to create disincentives to landowners' tolerance of permissive uses. Still, the courts' holdings in both of these categories of cases have tended to be contextual, and they do not always mesh into a restatement of a coherent set of rules.

The generation of public street rights by common law dedication, much like the formation of a contract, requires two steps to complete: an *offer* on the part of a property owner to dedicate property to some public use and an *acceptance* of that offer by some appropriate public authority. A landowner cannot unilaterally create a public street. In the early 1882 case of *Kennedy v. Williams*,[1] a landowner agreed with neighbors that if they helped him clear a pathway, it would become a public road. The neighbors did so, and the public began using the road, though no public authority assumed control over or maintained it. The North Carolina Supreme Court said that to create "a public highway, however originating, it must be a public charge, and must of necessity have an overseer and hands to work it; bridges erected when needed, and kept in repair at the public expense. And hence the law, in order to avoid an intolerable burden being thrown upon the public, will not permit every citizen, of his own head and according to his own ideas of necessity, to establish a highway by a mere act of private dedication."[2] More recently, the court explained that "dedication to the public is complete only when the offer is accepted by the responsible public authority, and neither the burdens nor benefits with attendant duties may be imposed on the public unless in some proper way it has consented to accept and assume them."[3]

A municipality can extinguish an offer of dedication by rejecting it. In *Lee v. Walker*,[4] the state high court held that a municipality lost the opportunity to claim public rights in a road shown on a recorded plat because it had adopted a resolution relinquishing all right and title in any streets within its jurisdiction, a step it had earlier taken to avoid claims of maintenance obligations.[5]

2.1 Express Offer of Dedication and Acceptance

An offer of dedication can be made expressly with a signed document, much like any other offer to transfer rights to real estate. Local land use ordinances typically require a property owner to make such an offer by placing a signed certificate on a subdivision plat stating that a right of way shown on the plat is dedicated to public use. Local ordinances may require that the street created by the proposed dedication meet the minimum standards for the North Carolina Department of

---

1. 87 N.C. 6 (1882).
2. *Id.* at 8.
3. Wofford v. N.C. State Highway Comm'n, 263 N.C. 677, 683, 140 S.E.2d 376, 381 (1965).
4. 234 N.C. 687, 68 S.E.2d 664 (1952).
5. *Id.* at 696, 68 S.E.2d at 670.

Transportation's acceptance into the state road system, as well as any local design standards, before the offer might be accepted. A plat certificate is currently the most common form of an express offer of dedication.

In today's regulatory environment, most new municipal streets arise during a land use review, in which the municipality examines and approves the details of each proposed street. This review process does not automatically constitute acceptance, however. By statute, "The approval of a plat shall not be deemed to constitute or effect the acceptance by the city or public of the dedication of any street or other ground, public utility line, or other public facility shown on the plat."[6] Regulators are likely to check to be sure that all rights of way are designated as public or private on the plat. They may also require that a developer supply a performance bond to pay for completion of the roads should the developer default in its obligation. The developer and the municipality are best served by having careful, express agreement about the municipality's willingness to assume a right of way as a public street and about any conditions necessary to exercise that acceptance.

The clearest way to create a public street is with express acceptance of an express offer of dedication. As the North Carolina Court of Appeals summarized, "Express acceptance may take the form of, *inter alia*, a formal ratification, resolution, or order by proper officials, the adoption of an ordinance, a town council's vote of approval, or the signing of a written instrument by proper authorities."[7] Local regulations may require that final plats have a signature block for the appropriate municipal authority to indicate acceptance, which is signed before the plat is recorded. This may be as simple as language such as this:

> [Municipality] hereby accepts, for the use of the general public, the offer of public streets and easements shown on this plat, without being deemed to agree to open said streets or easements or to assume any maintenance responsibility for them.

Before signing such a certificate, the municipality will want to ensure that all of the streets and easements shown on the plat as being for future public use are those that meet the municipality's expectations. Another approach is to accept an offer of dedication by resolution, such as the following:

> [Municipality] accepts the dedication and the property as described in/ shown on [register of deeds recording information], in its present condition, as an easement. By accepting the dedication, [municipality] shall not be deemed to have opened or to have agreed to open the easement

---

6. Chapter 160A, Section 374 of the North Carolina General Statutes (hereinafter G.S.).

7. Bumgarner v. Reneau, 105 N.C. App. 362, 366–67, 413 S.E.2d 565, 569 (1992).

area as a public street, nor shall [municipality] be deemed hereby to have accepted any responsibility or liability for any road construction or maintenance or the installation of any utilities.

A state statute permits a municipality to accept the dedication of a platted street that is outside its limits but within its extraterritorial subdivision control jurisdiction.[8] The statute provides that such an acceptance does not impose maintenance responsibilities or liabilities on the municipality. With this statutory authority, a municipality can arrange for a dedication to public use that can later be opened by the municipality if the property comes within corporate limits, keeping open an option for the state to incorporate the right of way into its system. It also enables a municipality to prevent a developer from barring the public from access to a right of way accepted according to this statute.[9]

Another state statute prescribes how subdivisions outside municipal limits are to show the creation of a new street or a change to an existing street.[10] It also applies to subdivisions within municipal limits that are part of the comprehensive plan for the future development of a street system in coordination with the North Carolina Department of Transportation (DOT).[11] The statute requires that such streets shown on a subdivision plat be identified as either public or private and that those identified as public meet the state's road design standards. Approval from the DOT's Division of Highways must be obtained before the plat can be recorded. The compliant plat must be recorded prior to any conveyance of a lot, and conveyances must refer to the recorded plat. Streets that are identified as for future public use on a plat are "conclusively presumed" to have been offered for dedication to the public. Any installation of utilities within a right of way must also be approved by the Division of Highways. A subsection of the statute prohibits agreements for the sale of a lot in a subdivision to which the statute applies without a signed "subdivision streets disclosure statement" noting the status of all streets and compliance with the statutory requirements, with information specified by statute.[12]

One approach that municipalities have tried in order to increase their ability to control rights of way has been the use of a "catch-all" acceptance, in which a municipality adopts a resolution to the purported effect that "all rights of way heretofore offered for dedication are hereby accepted as public streets." While such a sweeping move may be a tempting way to maximize opportunities for adding new streets, action to exercise uncertain property rights carries significant risks. Such

---

8. G.S. 160A-374.

9. *See, e.g.,* Emanuelson v. Gibbs, 49 N.C. App. 417, 271 S.E.2d 557 (1980) (authorizing an injunction to keep a public way open).

10. G.S. 136-102.6.

11. G.S. 136-102.6(g).

12. G.S. 136-102.6(f).

an "acceptance" could unsettle the legal status of rights of way (1) that may be the subject of a claim as to an offer of dedication but (2) which the municipality has no reason to control. A purported catch-all acceptance also could give landowners a basis upon which to contend that the municipality has undertaken to open a right of way and maintain it, despite the case law holding that acceptance alone does not trigger such a duty. *Waterway Drive Property Owners' Association, Inc. v. Town of Cedar Point*[13] is an example of a case involving the kind of confusion that can result from a municipality trying to maximize its acceptance options without being entirely clear about the intended scope of its actions. A newly incorporated town gave its mayor authority to accept specifically identified offers of dedication—within which the subject street was not included—as well as a catch-all power to extend that authority to offers of dedication made within one month in the future. One year later, the town recorded what purported to be a notice of having previously accepted several streets, this time including the subject right of way. This notice was deemed ineffective. The North Carolina Court of Appeals said that it "merely notes a previous acceptance of which there is no express record."[14] The court also said that "the documents do nothing more than loosely establish an intent to accept, either prospectively or retrospectively. Because this is not evidence of actual acceptance, we find no express acceptance of the dedication."[15] The court found no other basis to conclude that a public street had been established before the offer of dedication was effectively withdrawn, and the road remained private, contrary to the town's wishes to add it to its road system.

Conceptually, a public street acquired through dedication and acceptance is a public right to an easement for continued use of someone's property as a street. The owner who offered it for dedication is presumed to benefit from the value the road adds to the lots that depend on it for access. The town is not free to convert the street easement into a different use without payment of compensation. In *Wooten v. Town of Topsail Beach*,[16] the town sought to use an unpaved part of an accepted right of way as a park. The state appeals court said that this action was not allowed within the rights already acquired by the town and that "the use of dedicated property may constitute misuse or diversion if the use is inconsistent with the purposes of the dedication or substantially interfere[s] with it."[17] Converting the space to a park would in effect be excluding the public from the use for which the offer of dedication was intended—as a street or an appurtenance to a street.

---

13. 224 N.C. App. 544, 737 S.E.2d 126 (2012).

14. *Id.* at 550, 737 S.E.2d at 132.

15. *Id.*

16. 127 N.C. App. 739, 493 S.E.2d 285 (1997).

17. *Id.* at 741, 493 S.E.2d at 287.

In *March v. Town of Kill Devil Hills*,[18] on the other hand, the court of appeals held that a town could open an unused portion of a dedicated and accepted street and include parking spaces within it because parking spaces were associated with its use as a street.[19]

2.2 Implied Offer of Dedication and Acceptance

An offer of dedication for a street can be made with actions that induce reliance on the implication that a right of way is to be kept open for public travel. Many of the state's roads originated in this way when developers laid out towns with building lots and streets without formal offers of dedication to public use. Rarely would there be any perceived need for formality because everyone probably wanted the road. When a public authority relies on such an implied offer of dedication, and installs and maintains a street, public rights attach and become enforceable at common law. Accordingly, once offered for dedication, the right of way becomes available for the municipality to add it to the network of public streets, "to be opened and subjected to regulation as the growth of the city demands."[20] The North Carolina Supreme Court explained that the offer of dedication is complete upon public installation and maintenance because "it is rather the intention of the owner than the length of time of the user which must determine the fact of the dedication."[21]

Today, local land use regulators usually ensure that essential additions to the street network for new subdivisions are clearly offered for dedication by the developer on an approved subdivision plat. Previously, many subdivisions were developed without such well-documented offers. Issues in such cases arise when the landowner, the municipality, or users have different ideas about the extent to which a right of way was meant to be open to the public. In some cases, the landowner objects to a municipality's action to open a right of way as a public street, claiming that it was never offered for dedication and was intended to be available for an alternative use in future development. In other cases, the municipality claims that the street became irrevocably public because an offer of dedication was already accepted. In either of these situations, the practical question is whether the municipality must pay the landowner to make the right of way public, as municipalities

---

18. 125 N.C. App. 151, 479 S.E.2d 252 (1997).

19. *Id.* at 153–54, 479 S.E.2d at 253–54.

20. Bailliere v. Atl. Shingle Cooperage & Veneer Co., 150 N.C. 627, 638, 64 S.E. 754, 759 (1909).

21. State v. Marble, 26 N.C. 318, 320 (1844).

have the power of eminent domain to create streets in exchange for just compensation.[22] If the taking has already occurred—that is, the right of way was put into public use without ever having been offered for dedication and without compensation—the landowner may be entitled to damages for that taking.[23]

A municipality's acquisition of a street by means of an implied offer of dedication requires the same two steps as an express acquisition: an offer of dedication and acceptance. Regardless of the landowner's wishes, private land cannot become a public street unless the municipality accepts it as such. The North Carolina Supreme Court explained: "A city or town may in its discretion accept or reject an offer of dedication; it has the right to determine where its streets shall be located. It may accept a part of a street and determine the width of the street, and the width need not conform to the offer of dedication."[24] Put another way, "Neither burden nor benefits may be imposed upon the public unless some agency authorized to do so has assumed responsibility under the offer of dedication."[25]

Once an offer of a street dedication is accepted, the municipality's interest in the street is an easement, with the underlying fee remaining with the dedicator unless the offer expressly was for the full fee interest. This presumption of conveyed rights follows from the same equities that cause courts to enforce an implied offer of dedication—the owner benefits from causing others to rely on public access, and it is that expectation that is enforced. As the North Carolina Supreme Court explained: "[T]he abutting owner is entitled to every right and advantage in that part of the street of which he owns the fee, not required by the public. The easement of the public is the right to use and improve the street for the purposes of a highway only."[26]

The early cases on implied offers of dedication and acceptance arose as land uses were intensifying in the industrial era. Many of the roads that had long been in use for horse and wagon travel became streets for automobiles, without records of express dedication. Disputes about whether a right of way was meant for incorporation into a municipality's street system arose as developers wanted to put land once meant for travel to a different use. In those early cases, the North Carolina Supreme Court said, in general, that an offer of dedication could be shown by "any act done by an owner which clearly shows such an intention on his part, and a

---

22. *See* Chapter 4 for a discussion of the eminent domain power.

23. *E.g.,* Dep't of Transp. v. Elm Land Co., 163 N.C. App. 257, 264–66, 593 S.E.2d 131, 135–38 (2004).

24. Wofford v. N.C. State Highway Comm'n, 263 N.C. 677, 683–84, 140 S.E.2d 376, 381 (1965) (acceptance of a subdivision street by county commissioners foreclosed the dedicator's right to bar the public from using the road).

25. Rowe v. City of Durham, 235 N.C. 158, 160, 69 S.E.2d 171, 172–73 (1952).

26. White v. Nw. N.C. R.R. Co., 113 N.C. 611, 613, 18 S.E. 330, 331 (1893) (quoting John Lewis, Law of Eminent Domain in the U.S. 113 (1888)).

subsequent use by the public."[27] Courts had to address whether particular actions or failures to act were enough to express such an intent.

The central consideration with an implied offer of dedication is what the grantor led lot owners to believe about road access. As the North Carolina Court of Appeals put it, "Just as for express dedication, the 'intent of the owner' is the most important consideration as to implied dedication."[28] The court of appeals has explained that a finding of an implied dedication requires proof that the landowner's acts "are such as would fairly and reasonably lead an ordinary prudent man to infer an intent to dedicate, and [when] they are so received and acted upon by the public, the owner cannot, after acceptance by the public, recall the appropriation."[29] This focus was illustrated in *Metcalf v. Black Dog Realty, LLC*,[30] in which the court of appeals held that a county could not use land as a public park when the owner had dedicated it for use as a courthouse and county offices. The court said that the owner's intent for the dedication—not the county's intent for property uses—was what mattered.[31]

The typical case about intent to make an offer of dedication involves a subdivision with interior roads as to which the developer made no explicit reference of public use on a recorded subdivision plat or in the deeds for lots in the subdivision. In those cases, an implied offer of dedication is, in general, deemed triggered upon the first sale of a lot with reference to a plat showing the interior roads. As the North Carolina Supreme Court explained, "The mere recording of a map is not an absolute, unconditional offer to the public to dedicate to its use the streets shown thereon. There must be a sale and conveyance of one or more of the lots shown upon the map by reference thereto, or some other manifestation of intent, to make the offer absolute. The recording of the map is a conditional offer, the condition being that one or more of the lots shown upon the map be sold and conveyed."[32]

An implied offer of dedication made by reference to a subdivision plat in a deed is deemed to include all public ways shown on that plat. The reference effectively makes the matters shown on the plat part of the deeded property description.[33] As the North Carolina Supreme Court explained, "The plan or scheme indicated on

---

27. Crump v. Mims, 64 N.C. 767, 769 (1870).

28. Metcalf v. Black Dog Realty, LLC, 200 N.C. App. 619, 640, 684 S.E.2d 709, 723 (2009).

29. Dep't of Transp. v. Elm Land Co., 163 N.C. App. 257, 266, 593 S.E.2d 131, 137 (2004) (quoting Tise v. Whitaker-Harvey Co., 146 N.C. 374, 376, 59 S.E. 1012, 1013 (1907)).

30. 200 N.C. App. 619, 684 S.E.2d 709 (2009).

31. *Id.* at 640–41, 723–24.

32. State Highway Comm'n v. Thornton, 271 N.C. 227, 234–35, 156 S.E.2d 248, 254 (1967).

33. Collins v. Asheville Land Co., 128 N.C. 563, 565, 39 S.E. 21, 22 (1901).

the map or plat is regarded as a unity, and it is presumed, as well it may be, that all the public ways add value to all the lots embraced in the general plan or scheme."[34]

The common law rule that results in the enforcement of streets shown on plats is a presumption, which can be defeated with unambiguous language in the deeds for affected subdivided lots. For example, in *Todd v. White*,[35] the owners of a large tract recorded a plat that showed lots, streets, and an area labeled as "park." They sold a number of lots by reference to the plat. The successor owners of the land that included the park filed a statutory withdrawal of the park area from public use, to which a lot owner objected. The deeds to lot owners included a reservation that the developers and their successors "shall have the right to change, alter or close up any street or avenue shown upon said map or plat not adjacent to the lot above described and not necessary to the full enjoyment by the party of the second part of the above described property *and shall retain the right and title to, and the control and disposition of all parks*, streets, avenues and planting spaces and areas within the boundaries . . . as shown on said map or plat, subject only to the rights of the party of the second part for the purposes of egress and ingress necessary to the full enjoyment of the above described property."[36] The state supreme court held that this language in the deeds "clearly reserved . . . the title and power to dispose of the Park area unburdened by easement for park purposes."[37]

The mere existence of a design showing a public street—without a conveyance based on it—is unlikely to be enough to establish public rights. In the early 1912 case of *Green v. Miller*,[38] the plaintiff purchased a lot without notice that it had been platted into lots and streets. Some lots were sold according to that plat configuration, but the plat was not recorded. There was conflicting information about whether there was physical evidence of any streets shown on the plat. The North Carolina Supreme Court was unpersuaded that the unrecorded plat was an offer of dedication that the municipality could accept. It stated: "[I]t is necessary that in some way notice of the dedication thus made be fixed upon those who may buy any part of the property which is subject to or charged with the easement, or of the rights of others flowing from the dedication. It would be unjust that a rule, which is based upon an equitable doctrine, should, in its application, deprive a man of property bought in good faith, for value, and without notice of the right to the easement."[39]

---

34. *Id.* at 566, 39 S.E. at 22.
35. 246 N.C. 59, 97 S.E.2d 439 (1957).
36. *Id.* at 62, 97 S.E.2d at 441 (emphasis added by court).
37. *Id.* at 63, 97 S.E.2d at 442.
38. 161 N.C. 25, 76 S.E. 505 (1912).
39. *Id.* at 30, 76 S.E. at 507.

Because the developers' intent is what matters most with an implied offer and acceptance, the plat need not be recorded if it is somehow otherwise incorporated into a conveyance. This may occur if deeds for lots refer to an unrecorded plat showing a public right of way.[40] In such a case, "Once a right of way dedication has taken place and becomes open to the public and at least part of the area is maintained, the period of use becomes immaterial and the dedication becomes irrevocable."[41] On the other hand, a street or other public dedication shown on a conceptual plat will not be an enforceable offer if lots were conveyed only according to different plans.[42]

An intent to dedicate to public use also can found within the contents of a developer's deeds of conveyance, such as when a sub-divider refers in deeds to an existing roadway that serves not only the grantee of the lot but also "members of the general public."[43] A developer's intent may be expressed in other instruments as well. For example, in *Kraft v. Town of Mt. Olive*,[44] the North Carolina Court of Appeals looked to a developer's history of conveyances to assess intent. The original owner of the right of way at issue made several conveyances referring to an alleyway to be kept open for public use. The current owner contested this public status and pointed to his deed, which had no reservation for general public use. The court instructed that the proper focus should be on the original developer's intent, which could be demonstrated by conveyances to others, even though not in the direct chain of title to the burdened lot.[45] In *Kraft*, additional evidence of an offer of dedication and acceptance included the fact that, for many years, the right of way owner was not taxed on the land; the land was in active public use; and the town paved it thirty years before the owner brought the challenge.[46]

A subdivision's configuration also can be a factor in determining whether the developer intended to offer rights of way for public dedication. A subdivision may be designed with a geometric lot arrangement and an interior strip that makes no sense other than as a public street. However, there must be a pattern showing an intent to make the road public.[47] For example, in *State Highway Commission*

---

40. Dep't of Transp. v. Haggerty, 127 N.C. App. 499, 501–02, 492 S.E.2d 770, 771–72 (1997).

41. *Id.* at 501, 492 S.E.2d at 772.

42. Stephens Co. v. Myers Park Homes Co., 181 N.C. 335, 339–43, 107 S.E. 233, 235–37 (1921); Sexton v. Elizabeth City, 169 N.C. 385, 389–94, 86 S.E. 344, 345–48 (1915).

43. Bumgarner v. Reneau, 105 N.C. App. 362, 364–67, 413 S.E.2d 565, 567–69 (1992).

44. 183 N.C. App. 415, 645 S.E.2d 132 (2007).

45. *Id.* at 419, 645 S.E.2d at 136.

46. *Id.* at 420–23, 645 S.E.2d at 136–38.

47. Town of Highlands v. Edwards, 144 N.C. App. 363, 368, 548 S.E.2d 764, 767 (2001).

v. Thornton,[48] the state built a road across private land to connect someone else's truck freight terminal to the highway system. A plat had been recorded sixteen years earlier showing a ten-lot subdivision with a driveway, but there was no indication that the driveway was intended as a public road. The North Carolina Supreme Court said that "it would be most unreasonable to suppose that the defendants, by recording their map of their land, intended, irrespective of whether they ever sold any part of their property, to give to the public the right to drive at will, in and out of their property over this 'dead end' strip."[49]

Merely leaving an area unlabeled on a subdivision plat also is unlikely to be deemed an offer of dedication of that space to public use. In *Cooper v. United States*,[50] a North Carolina federal court, finding no controlling state law, held that "an unlabeled space on a plat indicates a reservation in the property owner rather than a dedication."[51] According to the federal court, an open space without detail is not enough to meet the requirement of showing "acts 'unmistakable in their purpose and decisive in their character'" that can constitute an offer of dedication to public use.[52]

An intent to dedicate also is contradicted by uses that consistently demonstrate that the land was intended to be private, such as when the owner of the land pays taxes on it and authorizes a utility to install lines within it.[53] However, developers will have difficulty denying a finding of implied intent to dedicate rights of way on property they are developing if they remain silent while the municipality maintains roads or installs utility lines on that property.[54]

A North Carolina statute provides a method for abutters of property in dispute to bring a special proceeding to get a court declaration that a right of way on that property is public.[55] At least two-thirds of landowners with frontage on the right of way must join in the action; the right of way must be shown on an unrecorded plat; the right of way must have been actually opened and used by the public; and at least three of the abutters' deeds must "recite the existence of the right of way as a named street or road."[56] When these conditions are met, the clerk of superior

---

48. 271 N.C. 227, 156 S.E.2d 248 (1967).

49. *Id.* at 235, 156 S.E.2d at 254.

50. 779 F. Supp. 833 (E.D.N.C. 1991).

51. *Id.* at 836.

52. *Id.* (quoting Nicholas v. Salisbury Hardware & Furniture Co., 248 N.C. 462, 468, 103 S.E.2d 837, 842 (1958) (quoting Emory Washburn, A Treatise on the American Law of Easements and Servitudes 188 (3d ed. 1873))).

53. Dep't of Transp. v. Elm Land Co., 163 N.C. App. 257, 266, 593 S.E.2d 131, 137–38 (2004).

54. Dep't of Transp. v. Haggerty, 127 N.C. App. 499, 502, 492 S.E.2d 770, 772 (1997).

55. G.S. 136-96.1.

56. *Id.*

court will issue an order declaring the right of way to be dedicated to public use.[57] In effect, this procedure simplifies abutters' burden of proof under narrow conditions, because the abutters need to establish specific elements in the statute rather than invoke unwieldy common law principles. Completion of the procedure does not mandate municipal maintenance of any right of way.

2.3 Offers of Dedication and Security Interests

In today's transactional environment, a dedication of land for use as a public street or utility easement is likely to be part of a subdivision development for which a lender is providing secured financing. In such cases, the lender's consent to the subdivision will be part of the lending process, and the lender will expect to give release deeds for the subdivided lots, as they are sold, with the benefit of the street and utility easements. The secured lender will have no reason to object to, and will most likely insist upon, public dedications made according to the subdivision plat. Accordingly, municipalities have no obvious reason to consider the need for getting a lender's explicit agreement to a dedication. There is a possibility, however, that complications could arise regarding the effectiveness of an offer of dedication made without the lender's consent, especially if the project fails and the lender looks to sell the land at foreclosure to someone who wants to develop it without the streets or easements shown on an earlier subdivision plat.

The potential for an issue regarding the viability of an offer of dedication to arise after foreclosure is due to the priority rights of a holder of a recorded security interest in land. As the North Carolina Supreme Court explained, "Ordinarily, all encumbrances and liens which the mortgagor or trustor imposed on the property subsequent to the execution and recording of the senior mortgage or deed of trust will be extinguished by sale under foreclosure of the senior instrument."[58] A purchaser at a foreclosure sale acquires all the rights conveyed in the deed of trust or mortgage, which are superior to attempted conveyances by the owner after the security interest was already given.

An issue about the effect of a foreclosure on an offer of dedication arose in the North Carolina Court of Appeals case *Tower Development Partners v. Zell,*[59] in which a landowner claimed that a lender could foreclose free of public rights in a road shown on a subdivision plat. The court said, "When the mortgagee gives

---

57. G.S. 136-96.1(b).
58. Dixieland Realty Co. v. Wysor, 272 N.C. 172, 175, 158 S.E.2d 7, 10 (1967).
59. 120 N.C. App. 136, 461 S.E.2d 17 (1995).

implied consent to the dedication by releasing lots sold referring to the plat which dedicates the streets, then the dedication is enforceable."[60] Courts in other jurisdictions similarly have found reasons to enforce offers of dedication despite foreclosure based on the nature of the development. As the Montana Supreme Court summarized, "It is apparent from an examination of the cases in other jurisdictions that certain fact situations arise which bring forth the application of estoppel and similar doctrines which prevent the application" of the general rule that a mortgagor cannot affect a mortgagee's rights with a dedication to which the mortgagee did not consent.[61] As an Illinois court said, "The mortgagee's assent will be implied where it recognizes the plat as having been properly made, sells lots pursuant to the plat and executes releases therefor."[62] A Florida court explained, a mortgagee who releases lots in this manner "must be held to have concurred in and to be estopped from now questioning the dedication of the streets."[63] As the Illinois court explained, without this implied assent requirement, "lots would be 'valueless and unsalable' because there would be no means of ingress or egress to them."[64] Other courts have held that a secured lender's consent to a subdivision implies consent "to laying out the usual streets and alleys."[65]

To head off potential complications regarding the enforceability of an offer of dedication on property subject to a recorded security interest, a municipality can insist that the owner obtain and record with the register of deeds an explicit consent from the holder of the security interest. For instance, the consent could state the following:

> The undersigned, now the secured creditor in the deed of trust with an original grantor of _____, recorded at Book _____, Page _____ at the _____ County Register of Deeds, North Carolina, consents to the dedication, for the benefit of the public, of streets and easements shown on the plat recorded at Plat Book _____, Page _____ of the _____ County Register of Deeds, North Carolina, and releases from the lien of the above-identified deed of trust those portions of the property dedicated for public use, which release shall not affect the lien of the deed of trust upon the other land not released hereby.

---

60. *Id.* at 142, 461 S.E.2d at 21.
61. Descheemaeker v. Anderson, 310 P.2d 587, 591 (Mont. 1957).
62. Republic Bank of Chi. v. Vill. of Manhattan, 32 N.E.3d 1141, 1150 (Ill. App. Ct. 2015).
63. Weills v. City of Vero Beach, 119 So. 330, 332 (Fla. 1928).
64. *Republic Bank of Chi.*, 32 N.E.3d at 1150.
65. Smith v. Heath, 102 Ill. 130, 138 (1882).

Effective consent results in enforceability of the specific public rights intended by the property owner while maintaining the secured lender's power of foreclosure as to the rest of the property, including the right to sell at foreclosure any lots not released from the security interest.

2.4 Withdrawal and Abandonment of Offers of Dedication

A common theme in disputes about offers of dedication is the contention that, if an offer was even made, it has since been withdrawn or abandoned and, therefore, a municipality can no longer accept it. Several questions about public rights might result from this contention. A different, though related, question is whether, in this situation, individual lot owners have an irrevocable right to use a right of way themselves. As described in section 2.5, *infra*, a developer's representation of unrestricted road access on a plat becomes irrevocable *with respect to the lot owners* when the developer makes the first conveyance to a lot owner who relies on that representation. However, the fact that a lot owner has a private right of access does not necessarily mean that a municipality has a continuing right to convert the right of way into a public street.[66]

The mere passage of time will not cause an offer of dedication to expire.[67] Statutes have long provided that a municipality is deemed to have abandoned an offer of dedication after a certain number of years have passed, at which time the property owner can withdraw the offer with a publicly recorded notice. This process enables a developer to clear claims of continued public rights that have not been exercised within a reasonable time. The limitations period was once twenty years according to legislation enacted in 1921.[68] Current law, G.S. 136-96, establishes a statutory procedure by which a plat dedicator may withdraw an offer of dedication if the street at issue is not "actually opened and used by the public" within fifteen years. Under the statute, after this time period has run, the offer of dedication is "conclusively presumed to have been abandoned by the public for the purposes for which same shall have been dedicated," but the presumption does not attach until a declaration of withdrawal has been filed and recorded in the register of deeds' office. In other words, until the declaration is filed, the public authorities may accept and open the street, even if the offer is more than fifteen years old. The statutory right to withdraw does not apply if the right of way is a future street

---

66. Irwin v. City of Charlotte, 193 N.C. 109, 113, 136 S.E. 368, 371 (1927).
67. Roberts v. Town of Cameron, 245 N.C. 373, 376, 95 S.E.2d 899, 901 (1957).
68. 1921 N.C. Sess. Laws ch. 174.

that is part of a state comprehensive transportation plan developed pursuant to G.S. 136-66.2.[69]

Only the developer who offered the dedication, or that developer's successor in title, may file the declaration to withdraw the offer under the statute.[70] The subject subdivision's lot owners do not have the power to do so.[71] There is no such right to withdraw under the statute "in any case where the continued use of any strip of land dedicated for street or highway purposes shall be necessary to afford convenient ingress or egress to any lot or parcel of land sold and conveyed by the dedicator of such street or highway."[72] This would apply when the right of way is the only route connecting a lot to a public street,[73] but the question of whether an alternative route is "convenient" can be subject to dispute. The North Carolina Supreme Court has restated the question as "whether the street is reasonably necessary for the use of" a lot.[74] Reasonableness is a familiar concept in easement law in general. Because the law of dedication and acceptance is based on a developer's promise to connect lot owners to a public road, [75] a lot owner should not be relegated to an alternative route that would have made no sense in the original development. A lot owner may not be able to oppose the withdrawal of an offer of dedication if there is another direct and open route to the public network, but the owner may be able to insist that the route remain open rather than be required to purchase rights to more land or install an alternative driveway at significant cost.

A municipality may reserve easements for its own utilities or for those of other utility companies in rights of way that a dedicator may withdraw.[76] To do so, the municipality must first give notice to the party with the power of withdrawal at least five days before a public hearing on the matter. The rights are reserved only if the municipality passes a resolution with a "declaration of retention of utility easements," specifically describing the retained easements, before a proper withdrawal is filed. The declaration must be recorded with the register of deeds.[77]

---

69. G.S. 136-96.

70. *Id.*; Town of Atl. Beach v. Tradewinds Campground, Inc., 97 N.C. App. 655, 657, 389 S.E.2d 276, 277-78 (1990).

71. Cavin v. Ostwalt, 76 N.C. App. 309, 312–13, 332 S.E.2d 509, 511 (1985).

72. G.S. 136-96.

73. Janicki v. Lorek, 255 N.C. 53, 59–60, 120 S.E.2d 413, 418 (1961).

74. Wofford v. N.C. State Highway Comm'n, 263 N.C. 677, 683, 140 S.E.2d 376, 381 (1965).

75. *See* Allen v. Duvall, 311 N.C. 245, 251, 316 S.E.2d 267, 271 (1984) (construing a claim to an easement that was not well delineated, the court said, "The law endeavors to give effect to the intention of the parties, whenever that can be done consistently with rational construction.").

76. G.S. 160A-299(g).

77. *Id.*

In rare situations, an offer of dedication shown on a plat may be deemed with-drawn regardless of the statutory process for withdrawal. This may occur if devel-opment has proceeded without regard to how the plat showed the subject right of way. An obvious withdrawal occurs when a developer re-plats a subdivision, changing the street and lot lines shown on the first plat, and all purchasers rely on the revised plat.[78] However, more subtle changes have resulted in a deemed with-drawal. For example, in the 1927 case of *Irwin v. City of Charlotte*,[79] a recorded plat showed part of a tract as a "park." A successor to the owner who recorded the plat acquired the tract and used it without regard to any such park, and he recorded a different plat showing the prior park notation to be a mistake. There was evi-dence that the municipality refused to accept the park when the plat showing it was recorded. Despite these changed circumstances, the municipality later sought to devote the area to use as a public park, even though the owner occupied it for other purposes for more than twenty years. The North Carolina Supreme Court held that there could be no public rights to such a park if no purchasers had relied on its existence.[80]

Affirming the trial court, the supreme court reached a similar result about with-drawal based on changed circumstances a few years later in *Gault v. Town of Lake Waccamaw*,[81] which involved developer-recorded deeds referring to a plat that showed streets and other public spaces. The developer's successor in title closed off a space shown as a public square on the plat and devoted it to exclusively private use. The subdivision was later incorporated into a municipality, which insisted that it had accepted all spaces shown as public on the plat. The court held that what the plat showed was a commitment to the lot owners, who could have insisted that the space be kept open. After twenty years of adverse possession, however, this right was lost. The court held that the municipality, which did not exist when an offer of public dedication was made, did not have a right to accept the offer later.[82] Reading this case as an implied offer of dedication, the holding is consistent with the notion that the grantor's intent controls, and a grantor could not have intended to dedicate to a municipality that did not exist.

Other circumstances can end the possibility of municipal acceptance of what once appeared to be an offer of dedication. When a street has not yet been accepted or put to use, an implied offer of dedication shown on a plat can be withdrawn from both public and lot owner use if the subdivision is reconfigured and the developer gets the lot owners' consent to the reconfiguration. As the North Carolina Supreme

---

78. Sexton v. Elizabeth City, 169 N.C. 385, 393, 86 S.E. 344, 347 (1915).
79. 193 N.C. 109, 136 S.E. 368 (1927).
80. *Id.* at 113, 136 S.E. at 370–71.
81. 200 N.C. 593, 158 S.E. 104 (1931).
82. *Id.* at 601–03, 158 S.E. 109–10.

Court said, an offer of dedication "is deemed to be recalled by deed in repudiation of the plat, and, at times, by deed conveying the land as an entirety without reference to the plat or any recognition of it and a user, according to the terms and intent of the deed."[83] In *Rowe v. City of Durham*,[84] a developer had recorded a subdivision plat showing streets outside the city's corporate limits. When the land was incorporated into the city, the city attempted to accept a small tract shown on the plat for extension of an existing road. The developer had already conveyed that tract by metes and bounds. The state supreme court held that the tract was effectively withdrawn from the offer by the conveyance before the city had any authority to accept it.[85] *Rowe* illustrates that acceptance can only occur if a municipality has the power to accept while the offer of dedication remains viable. Similarly, in *Town of Farmville v. A.C. Monk & Co.*,[86] the North Carolina Supreme Court held that a town could not accept an offer of dedication (for street purposes) made before the town was incorporated and the land was conveyed without any reference to a map on which the alleged street was shown.[87]

A municipality may be able to demonstrate that an offer of dedication was already accepted—and therefore can no longer be withdrawn—if the municipality has treated the right of way as public without any contrary intervention from the developer. As the state court of appeals summarized, "Acceptance may be manifested not only by maintenance and use as a public street, but by official adoption of a map delineating the area as a street, followed by other official acts recognizing its character as such."[88] In *Tower Development Partners v. Zell*,[89] for example, the appeals court held that acceptance occurred after a street had been paved for two years, a plat showing it as public had been adopted into the municipality's official zoning map, and the property was removed from the municipality's tax listing.[90] In *White v. Northwest Property Group—Hendersonville #1, LLC*,[91] the court held that a connector roadway became public when the municipality involved incorporated a plat showing the roadway into its zoning ordinance, entered into a cost-sharing agreement with the developer for the roadway's construction, and agreed to maintain it after it was built to specifications.[92] The North Carolina Court of Appeals noted, "A zoning map is one type of official map that may

---

83. Wittson v. Dowling, 179 N.C. 542, 546, 103 S.E. 18, 19–20 (1920).
84. 235 N.C. 158, 69 S.E.2d 171 (1952).
85. *Id.* at 160–62, 69 S.E.2d at 172–73.
86. 250 N.C. 171, 108 S.E.2d 479 (1959).
87. *Id.* at 176–79, 108 S.E.2d at 483–85.
88. Tower Dev. Partners v. Zell, 120 N.C. App. 136, 141, 461 S.E.2d 17, 21 (1995).
89. 120 N.C. App. 136, 461 S.E.2d 21 (1995).
90. *Id.* at 141–42, 462 S.E.2d at 21.
91. 225 N.C. App. 810, 739 S.E.2d 572 (2013).
92. *Id.* at 815–19, 739 S.E.2d at 576–79.

delineate a public road."[93] In cases such as these, official maps showing roads as public originated in a planning process that amounted to at least some evidence of the developer's intent that the disputed area become a public street. In each case the municipality did not generate these maps unilaterally, without the developer's involvement.

Acceptance and use of a portion of a single street constitutes acceptance of the entire street, ending the possibility of withdrawal of any portion.[94] As the North Carolina Court of Appeals said in a 1940 case, "the unused portion has not, by reason of nonuse, lost the character of a street for which it was originally dedicated."[95] In a more recent case, the court of appeals instructed that where a portion of a dedicated street was accepted, the unaccepted portion remains "dedicated to public use, 'though not kept in repair by the town, and is not to be obstructed because it must at all times be free to be opened as occasion may require.'"[96] The courts presume that all public ways shown as dedicated on a subdivision plat are a unity and that they add value in some way to the subdivision lots.[97] Accordingly, an owner may not use the statutory procedure of G.S. 136-96 to withdraw a portion of an accepted right of way that has not been opened through improvement and maintenance. The North Carolina Supreme Court emphasized, "It is now well settled [that] the dedication of a street may not be withdrawn, if the dedication has been accepted and the street *or any part of it* is actually opened and used by the public."[98]

The situation where a municipality accepts an offer of dedication based on a plat that shows a public use is to be distinguished from the cases in which no action was taken based on a plat showing a public use and lot owners never relied on any part of the right of way as shown on that plat. This distinction was illustrated in the 1940 case of *Home Real Estate Loan & Ins. Co. v. Town of Carolina Beach*,[99] which involved a developer who recorded a plat showing a street ninety-nine feet wide and who sold some lots with reference to it. None of the lots that were sold abutted the street shown on the plat. The developer later recorded a different plat narrowing the road to eighty feet, and lots were sold using that revised layout.

---

93. *Id.* at 816, 739 S.E.2d at 576.

94. Home Real Estate Loan & Ins. Co. v. Town of Carolina Beach, 216 N.C. 778, 785–86, 7 S.E.2d 13, 19 (1940).

95. *Id.* at 787, 7 S.E.2d at 20.

96. Town of Oriental v. Henry, 197 N.C. App. 673, 679, 678 S.E.2d 703, 707 (2009) (quoting *Home Real Estate Loan & Ins. Co.*, 216 N.C. at 788, 7 S.E.2d at 20).

97. Hughes v. Clark, 134 N.C. 457, 462, 46 S.E.2d 956, 958 (1904).

98. Food Town Stores v. City of Salisbury, 300 N.C. 21, 29, 265 S.E.2d 123, 129 (1980) (quoting Russell v. Coggin, 232 N.C. 674, 62 S.E. 2d 70 (1950) (emphasis added by the court)).

99. 216 N.C. 778, 7 S.E.2d 13 (1940).

The developer also recorded a declaration withdrawing the width not included within the revised layout. The North Carolina Supreme Court held that once the developer sold lots with reference to the original plat, the ninety-nine-foot layout was irrevocably dedicated to the lot owners' use.[100] In other words, the municipality's discretion to accept the offer of dedication to open a road narrower than the offer did not affect the lot owners' rights to full use.

2.5 Subdivision Lot Rights without Acceptance

Municipal acceptance of an offer to dedicate a right of way for street purposes gives the local government control to ensure that the street will be kept up to its standards. Of course, such acceptance also brings with it costs and responsibilities. Most subdivision lot owners want a municipality to take over the subdivision's roads, and many of the cases involving implied dedication and acceptance were brought by such owners. They typically allege that they bought their lots relying on the developer's promises about good streets, and the cases focus on the reasonableness of that reliance, as well as on the actions of the municipality to accept public responsibility. In circumstances in which the municipality has not taken control over a road, the case law recognizes that lot owners nonetheless may have a right to keep a subdivision road open when they have relied on the developer's express or implied promise of such use. Although in such cases lot owners will not have the benefit of municipal maintenance, they seek a protected means of travel and may be able to organize an association for private maintenance.

Since automobile travel began, the North Carolina Supreme Court has held that a conveyance to lot owners that refers to use of a right of way shown on a plat will include a continued right to such use.[101] As the North Carolina Court of Appeals explained, "Creation of an implied easement by plat is grounded in principles of estoppel; the easement is created because a grantee purchases property in reliance on a right of way or other easement reflected in the plat at the time of the conveyance."[102] This right exists regardless of whether the government takes control over the right of way as a public street, which is a legal status that only a municipality can establish.[103] The North Carolina Supreme Court said that "where lots are sold and conveyed by reference to a map or plat which represents a division of a tract

---

100. *Id.* at 787, 7 S.E.2d at 19.
101. Davis v. Morris, 132 N.C. 435, 436, 43 S.E. 950, 951 (1903).
102. Town of Carrboro v. Slack, 820 S.E.2d 527, 534 (N.C. App. 2018).
103. Nelms v. Davis, 179 N.C. App. 206, 211, 632 S.E.2d 823, 827 (2006).

of land into subdivisions, streets and lots, such streets become dedicated to the public use, and the purchaser of a lot or lots acquires the right to have all and each of the streets kept open, and it makes no difference whether the streets be in fact open or accepted by the governing board of the towns or cities if they lie within municipal corporations."[104]

Any purchaser of a lot with the benefit of a subdivision right of way may bring a court action for an injunction to keep it open.[105] The nature of the lot owner's interest in the platted streets is narrow and largely negative. It is a right of use that is protected. The lot owner's interest does not entitle the owner to demand that any road shown on the plat actually be constructed, not even the road on which the owner's lot is located. Absent an agreement to the contrary, the general rule is that the owner of the land over which an easement runs has no duty to maintain the easement for the benefit of owners with a right to its use.[106] Rather, the lot owner is merely entitled to enjoin the obstruction of use of the road[107] or to enjoin sales for purposes inconsistent with street uses.[108] The right to keep a right of way free of obstructions may include a right to remove trees that prevent a lot owners' use of the land as a right of way.[109]

As noted in section 2.2, *supra*, a municipality likely cannot effectively accept a road shown on a plat when the plat had nothing to do with the actual development of the subdivision. The same is true for lot owners who want to claim rights based on such a plat. The lot owners' right to insist that subdivision roads be kept open can be lost when uses evolve in such a way that contradict the premise that the owners relied on such availability. The North Carolina Supreme Court said that "purchasers . . . may lose their right to have streets and alleys opened by permitting them to be occupied and used adversely for more than twenty years for purposes inconsistent with their use as streets and alleys."[110] In the early case of *State Co. v. Finley*,[111] lot owners were unable to insist on the use of roads shown on a layout that was never developed, as to which the town disclaimed any interest in its streets and alleys, on land that was laid out and developed differently.[112]

The easement derived by implication from a subdivision is only for the benefit of owners of lots who were part of the subdivision and who relied on the easement

104. Hughes v. Clark, 134 N.C. 457, 462, 46 S.E. 956, 958 (1904).

105. Broocks v. Muirhead, 223 N.C. 227, 232, 25 S.E.2d 889, 892 (1943).

106. Tanglewood Prop. Owners' Ass'n v. Isenhour, 803 S.E.2d 453, 459–60 (N.C. Ct. App. 2017).

107. *Broocks*, 223 N.C. at 232–33, 25 S.E.2d at 892–93.

108. Conrad v. W. End Hotel & Land Co., 126 N.C. 776, 776, 36 S.E. 282, 283 (1900).

109. Stanley v. Laughter, 162 N.C. App. 322, 327–28, 590 S.E.2d 429, 433 (2004).

110. Lee v. Walker, 234 N.C. 687, 695, 68 S.E.2d 664, 669 (1952).

111. 150 N.C. 726, 64 S.E. 772 (1909).

112. *Id*. at 728–29, 64 S.E. at 773–74.

right's inclusion when purchasing their lots. The owner of the land may install a gate or other improvements to prevent trespassers, as long as the barriers do not prevent reasonable use by the lot owners with a right of access.[113] Owners outside the subdivision only acquire rights if the roads are accepted as public streets.[114] As the North Carolina Court of Appeals explained, the general public "only acquires rights in a dedication upon acceptance of the dedication. The reason such a dedication is not complete until acceptance is to prevent landowners, simply by executing a deed, from compelling the authorities to assume the burdens of maintaining or repairing property offered for dedication."[115]

113. Town of Carrboro v. Slack, 820 S.E.2d 527, 534 (N.C. Ct. App. 2018).
114. Owen v. Elliott, 258 N.C. 314, 318, 128 S.E.2d 583, 586 (1962).
115. Price v. Walker, 95 N.C. App. 712, 716, 383 S.E.2d 686, 688 (1989).

3

Acquisition by Public Use without an Offer of Dedication and Acceptance

A public street's origins cannot always be traced back to a developer's express offer of dedication and a municipality's acceptance of it. Sometimes the public has used a right of way for many years as if it were a street, with no evidence showing a developer's intent to dedicate it to such use. Under these circumstances, disputes may arise if the developer, or the developer's successor, wants to make different use of the land over which the right of way has run. To resolve these disputes, the courts apply the common law of prescriptive easements, an area of the law that can be confounding in general and especially thorny when the claim involves converting the right of way for general public use.

For decades, courts have made presumptions about the public's continued right of use to a given street based on long use without any interference from the landowner. For instance, in the early 1841 case of *Woolard v. McCullough*,[1] the North Carolina Supreme Court held that a six-mile stretch of road could be deemed public after it had "for more than twenty years been reputed to be, and had been used as, a public road."[2] The court said that "if the owner of land permit the public to pass and repass over his soil, and use it as a public highway, without molestation, or any assertion of his rights for some time, the law will presume a dedication of the way to general use."[3] Another legal presumption once applied to questions about the existence of a public road was the notion of a "lost grant"; that is, if there has been uncontested public use for a long time, then there must have been a documented—though unrecorded—conveyance of such rights. For example, in an 1854 case, the North Carolina Supreme Court said: "[T]he right of the public must be evidenced by an actual grant unless the road has been used as a common highway for more than twenty years, in which case no deed need be produced, as one will be presumed, that is, it will be presumed that a deed was actually executed, and was, of course, formerly in existence, but now is lost. The proof of the existence of the road in the present case depends upon this common law presumption; and the easement claimed and enjoyed by the public is founded upon the same well-known principle which supports private prescriptive rights."[4]

---

1. 23 N.C. 432 (1841).
2. *Id.* at 436.
3. *Id.*
4. Tarkington v. McRea, 47 N.C. 48, 49–50 (1854) (citation omitted).

The essence of this "well-known principle which supports private prescriptive rights" is that there comes a time when a property owner ought to have done something about others using a portion of that property the owner now claims to have been exclusive.[5] As the *Restatement of Property—Servitudes* characterizes it, "Prescription doctrine rewards the long-time user of property and penalizes the property owner who sleeps on his or her rights. In its positive aspect, the rationale for prescription is that it rewards the person who has made productive use of the land, it fulfills expectations fostered by long use, and it conforms titles to actual use of the property."[6]

Presumptions about lost deeds made sense in the 1800s, when highways were a welcome connection for travel. In fact, in both of the cases described above, in which the court expressed presumptions of owner grants, the owners were not contesting the public's right to a road, but rather a legal obligation to send labor to work on it, as was often required in that era.[7] Also, in the early 1800s, artificial presumptions were a common part of formal legal pleadings.[8] However, over time the presumptions of the old cases were apparently too much of an unnecessary fiction, while the enforceability of a prescriptive easement acquired through long-term use continued to be recognized.

The principles of prescriptive easements are fundamentally the same, whether the easement is for the benefit of individual users or for the public generally, but their application has special considerations when the claimed use is public. Although in a modern context of intensified land uses and regulated development a claim based on actual public use is less likely to arise than in earlier times, disputes still arise, and the possibility of permanent rights based solely on use creates dynamics that can surprise landowners, municipalities, and the traveling public. As with cases in which there is a dispute about an offer of dedication and acceptance, the courts have been inclined to uphold a municipality's control over a right of way that has been exercised without objection, and, without such a history of control, the courts tend to be more protective of private ownership.

---

5. Rogers v. Mabe, 15 N.C. 180, 188–89 (1833).

6. RESTATEMENT (THIRD) OF PROPERTY—SERVITUDES § 2.17 cmt. c (1998).

7. *Tarkington*, 47 N.C. at 48; *Woolard*, 23 N.C. at 436–37.

8. *See* Draper v. Conner & Walters Co., 187 N.C. 18, 20, 121 S.E. 29, 30 (1924) (discussing the use of presumptions in pleadings).

3.1 Public Prescriptive Easements Generally

A claim to a prescriptive easement is based on long-term use contrary to the property owner's right of exclusivity. The North Carolina Supreme Court identified four elements that a claimant must prove to establish a prescriptive easement:

> (1) that the use is adverse, hostile or under claim of right; (2) that the use has been open and notorious such that the true owner had notice of the claim; (3) that the use has been continuous and uninterrupted for a period of at least twenty years; and (4) that there is substantial identity of the easement claimed throughout the twenty-year period.[9]

A right of continued use under these circumstances is not settled until a court determines that the claimant has proved all four elements. This is difficult; courts are appropriately hesitant to derogate exclusive ownership rights from a landowner who tolerates neighbors' occasional uses. As the North Carolina Supreme Court said, "The modern tendency is to restrict the right of one to acquire a prescriptive right-of-way whereby another, through a mere neighborly act, may be deprived of his property by its becoming vested in one whom he favored."[10]

While the North Carolina courts are protective of a landowner's property rights, they also will find that prescriptive rights exist when the landowner acquiesced to what was an obvious and continuous use in a manner that looks to be a claim of right. Unlike an express or implied offer of dedication, the focus with a prescriptive claim is not on what the landowner apparently intended at the start of public use, but rather what the landowner failed to do during a long course of such use. The kind of adverse use that will be enough to establish a public street depends on the nature of the property being used and the way it has been used. No one can acquire prescriptive rights merely by occasionally entering another person's property or by entering it secretively. Nor can prescriptive rights arise based on a use to which the claimant is otherwise entitled.

To establish prescriptive rights, the use must be what is deemed "continuous." Without this characteristic, an owner is unlikely to have been put on notice that users were becoming settled in a claim of entitlement. A use that is interrupted by the owner, or abandoned by the user, will not be sufficient, but a use that is regular although not constant may be sufficient. To establish a prescriptive easement, there also must be a "substantial identity" of the path of use over time. In some circumstances, slight interruptions or deviations may not undercut the apparent nature of the users' claim of right. As the North Carolina Supreme Court said in

---

9. Potts v. Burnette, 301 N.C. 663, 666, 273 S.E.2d 285, 287–88 (1981).

10. *Id.* at 667, 273 S.E.2d at 288 (quoting 2 G. Thompson, Real Property § 335, at 145 (1980)).

a case involving a claim for access to the shore, "The fact that the portion of the easement claimed, which was marked and then paved by defendant, varies slightly from the old pathway does not, in and of itself, defeat the claim of a prescriptive easement over that portion of the pathway. Changes made to suit the convenience of the owner of the subservient land during the prescriptive period do not destroy the identity of the road claimed."[11] The court explained that determining whether an interruption defeats the establishment of a prescriptive right "depends upon the nature of the right and the attendant circumstances."[12]

3.2 Impermissive Use

Difficult cases involving claims to prescriptive rights can arise when a landowner has reason to contend that permission was given for the use at issue. A landowner's permission means that users cannot establish the element "that the use is adverse, hostile or under claim of right."[13] Courts have consistently held that a permissive use, no matter how long in duration or how often exercised, cannot ripen into an easement by prescription. If this were not the rule, landowners would risk losing property rights merely by the neighborly act of allowing others to cross their lands. Still, application of this principle is often problematic because it seems to put tolerant landowners at risk if users will not agree that the use in dispute is permissive—or if there is no simple way to reach such agreement, as may be the case with public use.

When analyzing whether a pattern of use is sufficiently adverse to create prescriptive rights, subjective intent is immaterial—the apparent nature of the use is what matters. Rights are obtained only when a landowner can fairly be expected to have objected to the continued use. The nature of the use must be such as to show that the owner knew, or ought to have known, that the right was being exercised not in reliance upon the owner's toleration or permission, but without regard to consent. As the North Carolina Supreme Court said, "There must, then, be some evidence accompanying the user, giving it a hostile character and repelling the inference that it is permissive and with the owner's consent, to create the easement by prescription and impose the burden upon the land."[14] The court also explained

---

11. Concerned Citizens of Brunswick Cty. Taxpayers Ass'n v. State, 329 N.C. 37, 49, 404 S.E.2d 677, 684 (1991).

12. *Id.* at 53, 404 S.E.2d at 687 (quoting 2 G. THOMPSON, REAL PROPERTY § 347, at 249–50).

13. *Potts*, 301 N.C. at 666, 273 S.E.2d at 287.

14. Boyden v. Achenbach, 86 N.C. 397, 399 (1882).

that an "owner's quiet acquiescence, a simple act of neighborly courtesy, in the use of a way convenient to others, and not injurious to himself" does not alone trigger an obligation "needlessly to interpose and prevent the enjoyment of the privilege in order to "[keep] the preservation of the right of property unimpaired."[15]

The issue of who must prove landowner permission, or the absence of it, has been resolved in different ways among the states. The North Carolina Supreme Court is among the states that tend to put the greater burden on the user claiming to have established prescriptive rights. The court has explicitly declined to "adopt the rule, obtaining in the majority of jurisdictions, that the user is presumed to be adverse."[16] Noting that easement by prescriptive use "is not favored in the law," the court has explained that "the better-reasoned view [is] to place the burden of proving every essential element, including hostility, on the party who is claiming against the interests of the true owner."[17] The court has further noted that "'[t]he modern tendency is to restrict the right of one to acquire a prescriptive right-of-way whereby another, through a mere neighborly act, may be deprived of his property by its becoming vested in one whom he favored.' Thus, in order for plaintiffs to succeed in their claim, they must have shown sufficient evidence of the hostile character of their use to create an issue of fact for the jury."[18]

Formal notice need not be shown to prove that a use was impermissive. The North Carolina Supreme Court explained this point in the seminal case of *Dickenson v. Pake* as follows: "To establish that a use is 'hostile' rather than permissive, 'it is not necessary to show that there was a heated controversy, or a manifestation of ill will, or that the claimant was in any sense an enemy of the owner of the servient estate.' A 'hostile' use is simply a use of such nature and exercised under such circumstances as to manifest and give notice that the use is being made under a claim of right."[19] For example, users who make improvements to a route over which they travel may in effect be conveying notice of such a claim of right. Applying *Dickenson* in a later case, the North Carolina Supreme Court upheld a jury finding of a prescriptive easement to continued public use of a roadway that connected the plaintiffs' land and a cemetery to a state road. The court noted that the road had been in use for at least fifty years openly and continuously and that "[n]o permission has ever been asked or given. Plaintiffs, on at least one occasion, smoothed, graded and gravelled the road, and have, on other occasions, attempted to work on it. Although there was no evidence that plaintiffs thought they owned the road,

---

15. *Id.* at 398.

16. *Potts*, 301 N.C. at 666–67, 273 S.E.2d at 288.

17. *Id.* at 667, 273 S.E.2d at 288.

18. *Id.* (quoting 2 G. THOMPSON, REAL PROPERTY § 335, at 145 (1980)).

19. 284 N.C. 576, 580–81, 201 S.E.2d 897, 900 (1974) (quoting Dulin v. Faires, 266 N.C. 257, 260–61, 145 S.E.2d 873, 875 (1966) (citations omitted)).

there was abundant evidence that plaintiffs considered their use of the road to be a *right* and not a privilege."[20] The resolution of these kind of issues depends on the particular facts of a given case. In *Potts v. Burnette*, for example, the court held that the evidence was "sufficient to rebut the presumption of permissive use and to allow, but not compel, a jury to conclude that the road was used under such circumstances as to give defendants notice that the use was adverse, hostile, and under claim of right and that the use was open and notorious and with defendants' full knowledge and acquiescence."[21]

In the typical case in which a history of use was found to be hostile, the landowner took no action to contest the users' actions. Sometimes a landowner is able to protect exclusive rights by giving notice that the use will not be allowed. If the use continues despite this notice, the landowner may attempt to block the use physically or, if that cannot be done peaceably, seek a court injunction. The landowner who does not want to take these steps—and who may be willing to allow current use by permission—has less clear direction about what will be deemed enough to preserve the landowner's exclusive rights. Some have advised that once a hostile use has begun, a landowner cannot thereafter protect exclusive rights by giving permission for the use.[22] The North Carolina Courts of Appeals has held, however, that when a landowner offers permission after the use has begun, there are circumstances in which the burden shifts back to the users to establish hostility by more than mere continued use.

In *Jones v. Miles*,[23] a claimant to a permanent easement maintained a driveway with decorative shrubbery on a neighbor's land. When a survey revealed the encroachment, the driveway users approached the neighbor and offered to purchase the disputed area. The neighbor refused to sell but said that the use could continue. Twelve years after this discussion, the user erected a fence in the area and installed a "no trespassing" sign. The neighbor responded with a correspondence describing the use as only permissive, reserving all rights, and stating that any claim of an interest in the property was unacceptable. The neighbor said to the encroaching user, "If you disagree that the driveway encroachment is not permissive and believe that the driveway encroachment is an open and hostile use by you . . . then you should inform me of that and prepare to remove the driveway encroachment as well."[24] Eventually, the users claimed that they had acquired own-

---

20. *Potts*, 301 N.C. at 668, 273 S.E.2d at 289 (emphasis in original).

21. *Id.*

22. James A. Webster, Jr., et al., Webster's Real Estate Law in North Carolina § 15-18[2] (6th ed. 2018) (emphasis in original) ("Permission given *after* the hostile use has begun does not destroy hostility.").

23. 189 N.C. App. 289, 658 S.E.2d 23 (2008).

24. *Id.* at 291, 658 S.E.2d at 25.

ership based on their use. The North Carolina Court of Appeals held, however, that upon receiving notice of the owner's reservation of rights, the users had to do more than ignore it. The court said that the owner's notice of permission required the users to take "affirmative steps" to put the owner "back on actual or constructive notice" of hostile intent, which did not occur until they erected the fence, and that the occupancy in this manner had not gone on for the required twenty years. The court said that "a true owner's grant of permission *will* defeat a possessor's hostile use if the possessor takes no further action to reassert his claim over the land. In such cases, the possessor has not put the true owner on notice that the possessor still intends to claim the disputed land as his own."[25] A dissenting judge disagreed with a rule that the record owner could stop the running of the hostile use period "simply by solely giving the party permission to use his property," arguing that "[o]nce adverse possession has begun and the owner is on notice, the burden shifts to the record owner to take physical or legal action to interrupt the running of the twenty year statutory period."[26]

Jones v. Miles shows that judges can have difficulty reconciling the common law rules for prescriptive easement claims. The parties involved in such claims are justifiably uncertain about who must do what to protect themselves when a user claims a continuing right and the owner is willing to tolerate that use but does not want to relinquish ownership rights permanently. From the users' perspective in *Jones*, a right of continued use might have been best protected by bringing litigation for a declaration that the record owner's permission was no longer required. However, an owner also takes a risk by not bringing litigation after becoming aware of a claim of right, as illustrated by the dissenting judge's view that the owner had "to take physical or legal action" to stop the use, not just give permission for it to continue.

3.3 Public Control and Maintenance

A distinctive feature of public prescription is that the use of a right of way to which such rights attach will not be restricted to particular lot owners who may have need of it. The issue of whether a right of way has become public most likely arises when the affected landowner looks to enforce a restriction against general use. Prescription is based on the notion that there comes a time when a landowner can no longer rightfully object to a use that has been obvious and claimed as a

---

25. *Id.* at 294, 658 S.E.2d at 27 (emphasis in original).
26. *Id.* at 298, 658 S.E.2d at 29 (Tyson, J., dissenting).

matter of right. For that right to have accrued to the public generally, the use needs to be such that the landowner knew it was being claimed in behalf of the public. Such a claim may have been obvious if a public authority had paved the subject street and maintained it. The cases more typically involve something less obviously public, however.

In the 1858 case *Davis v. Ramsey*, the North Carolina Supreme Court emphasized that something more than occasional use is necessary to establish a public prescriptive easement. When describing the evidence of right of way use in the case, the court said, "Many witnesses say that it has been used as a public road more than twenty years, but when their testimony is scrutinized, it amounts only to this: During all of that time the road has been open, and every person took the liberty of travelling over it who chose to do so. Such is the case with every private road in the country, so long as it remains open."[27] Noting a lack of evidence showing that a public authority had managed the road, the court said, "We do not decide that those facts are necessary to constitute a public road, although, under the provisions of our statutes, it is difficult to see how there can be a public road in our State without them . . . ."[28]

The North Carolina Supreme Court has regularly rejected claims to public prescriptive easements where there was no evidence of government control or maintenance of the property in dispute. Government involvement seems important for putting a landowner on notice that something more than a neighborly use is occurring. In an 1886 case, *Stewart v. Frink*, the North Carolina Supreme Court said: "The presumption of right in favor of the public, will not arise, unless the proper public authorities, as authorized by law, shall do something that puts the owner of the land on notice that his right is denied, and to assert the same by action, if he shall desire or see fit to do so. It would be unjust, as well as ungracious, to take advantage of his generous permission to use his land for public convenience, and the law will not allow this to be done."[29] Several years later, in *State v. Lucas*,[30] the court rejected a criminal complaint brought by the state against a landowner who had put up a fence to obstruct a path that the state said was a public road leading to a church. The court said that neighbors' occasional use of the right of way was insufficient to make it public, regardless of how long the use persisted.[31] In *Hemphill v. Board of Alderman*,[32] a municipality asked the court to declare that an alley was a public way based on a history of public use, where the only claim of

---

27. 50 N.C. 236, 240 (1858).
28. *Id.*
29. 94 N.C. 487, 487–88 (1886).
30. 124 N.C. 804, 32 S.E. 553 (1899).
31. *Id.* at 805–06, 32 S.E. at 553–54.
32. 212 N.C. 185, 193 S.E. 153 (1937).

maintenance or control involved a few isolated acts. The court found insufficient evidence of use except by permission and held that there could be no easement by prescription. The court said, "To establish the existence of a road or alley as a public way, in the absence of laying out by public authority or actual dedication, it is essential not only that there must be twenty years' use under claim of right adverse to the owner, but the road must have been worked and kept in order by public authority."[33]

Notwithstanding the importance ascribed to acts of public control as an element of proving a public prescriptive easement, the reported decisions have not always been entirely clear that such control is an essential element. In 1955, in *Scott v. Shackelford*,[34] the North Carolina Supreme Court noted that in some "old decisions" the court may have suggested that all that was required was evidence of use. The court attributed those suggestions to the difference in circumstances in early cases, in which presumptions were made because there was little formality and precision in the layout of public roads. The court said: "However, as the State and the towns developed, and larger and larger sums of money became available for highway and streets, they were surveyed with mathematical exactness. They were authorized by carefully prepared proceedings. Records of surveys and plats showing the exact location were made and were available at every courthouse and town hall. The authority for the location and construction can be ascertained without difficulty."[35] The court noted that these changes in conditions over the decades made the presumptions in the old cases less justifiable.[36] Summarizing the importance of its more recent decisions, the court said that "there can be in this State no public road or highway unless it be one either established by public authorities in a proper proceeding regularly instituted before the proper tribunal; or generally used by the public and *over which the public authorities have asserted control* for a period of twenty years or more; or dedicated to the public by the owner of the soil with the sanction of the authorities and *for the maintenance and operation of which they are responsible.*"[37] The court held as follows: "Now, it is not enough for the public to use the streets, highways or alleys for twenty years. The public authorities must assert control over them."[38] In a number of other cases, the North Carolina Supreme Court has rejected claims that a given right of way was

---

33. *Id.* at 188, 193 S.E. at 155.
34. 241 N.C. 738, 86 S.E.2d 453 (1955).
35. *Id.* at 743, 86 S.E.2d at 457.
36. *Id.*
37. *Id.* (quoting Chesson v. Jordan, 224 N.C. 289, 291, 29 S.E.2d 906, 908 (1944) (emphasis added by the court)).
38. *Id.*

public, noting that there was no proof that the public authorities exercised control over it or maintained it.[39]

Despite the prevailing theme in the cases that some evidence of public control and maintenance is required to establish a public street by prescription, there still have been some cases indicating otherwise, as noted by the North Carolina Supreme Court in *Scott v. Shackelford*, discussed above. In 1985, in *West v. Slick*, the North Carolina Supreme Court described the cases as "in conflict," noting that some early cases "fail to make any mention of public maintenance as an essential element, emphasizing, rather, use by the public for the requisite length of time and reputation of the road as a public way."[40] For instance, in 1920, in *Hoggard v. Mitchell*,[41] a landowner succeeded in establishing a claim that the public acquired a continued right to use an open space based on twenty years of use, occupation, and enjoyment as a matter of right. In that case, the state high court said that proof of control and maintenance was not always required, but rather "such an easement can be acquired by adverse user when the occupation is so general and of such a kind as to permit the inference and apprise an owner that the public has assumed control of his property and is exercising it as a matter of right."[42] The facts of the case, however, depicted circumstances much like an offer of dedication and acceptance, rather than prescriptive use without the developer's initial expression of intended dedication. The court noted, for example, that the developer's agent sold lots with reference to a plat that showed the disputed right of way as a street and made representations that it would be left open to the public.[43]

Some states recognize public prescriptive easements by statute with no showing of public maintenance required.[44] Others have the same rule by common law.[45]

---

39. *E.g.*, State v. Haynie, 169 N.C. 277, 282–83, 84 S.E. 385, 387 (1915) ("The proof in this case is that the public authorities had never exercised any control over this way and that it was not regarded, in any sense, as a public way . . . ."); State v. Fisher, 117 N.C. 733, 738, 23 S.E. 158, 158 (1895) (holding that the right of way at issue was not public and noting that the "best evidence" of a public claim would be "the fact that the proper authorities have appointed overseers and designated hands to work, and assumed for the public the responsibility of keeping the way in repair," all proving that it was regarded as public); State v. Purify, 86 N.C. 681, 682 (1882) (a road is public when the public keeps it in order and assumes responsibility for its reparation).

40. 313 N.C. 33, 53–56, 326 S.E.2d 601, 613–15 (1985).

41. 180 N.C. 255, 104 S.E. 561 (1920).

42. *Id.* at 261, 104 S.E. at 564.

43. *Id.* at 262, 104 S.E. at 565.

44. *E.g.*, Colo. Rev. Stat. § 43-2-201(1)(c) (2018) (declaring as public highways "all roads over private lands that have been used adversely without interruption or objection on the part of the owners of such lands for twenty consecutive years.").

45. *E.g.*, Elmer v. Rodgers, 214 A.2d 750, 752 (N.H. 1965) (citation omitted) ("[S]tabilization of long continued property uses has motivated the continued application of the doctrine of prescription based on the principles of statutes of limitation

This is the approach adopted in the *Restatement (Third) of Property—Servitudes*. Section 2.18 of the *Restatement* states what its reporters say is the better rule as follows: "Government bodies may acquire servitudes by dedication and condemnation, as well as by the methods [set forth in the rules for prescription]." Despite the confusion in the cases described above, such a rule would not follow naturally from North Carolina's case law. When the North Carolina cases are considered in context, there is no clear authority in this state for holding that a public right of way can be created by prescription based solely on use without any history of public authority control or maintenance. On balance, recent cases are to the contrary. For example, in the 1996 case *Wiggins v. Short*, the North Carolina Court of Appeals held that the evidence was insufficient to prove establishment of a public road when the only public maintenance of the road by the municipality involved was evidently work done in service of the municipality's own water drain easement.[46] In 2006, in *Wright v. Town of Matthews*, the state court of appeals put it succinctly when it said that for a right of way to become public by prescription, the "road must have been worked and kept in order by public authority."[47] The court held as insufficient disputed evidence that the state may have graded and graveled the road in the 1960s, which the court said was not the necessary "substantial, competent, and material evidence that the state maintained [the road] for the requisite twenty-year period."[48] In *Wright*, there was contradictory evidence that only occasional public maintenance occurred "as a courtesy to property owners due to damage by state equipment turning around."[49]

As a practical matter, today a municipality is unlikely to be confronted with the question of whether a public prescriptive easement can be established without evidence of any public authority control or maintenance. Ultimately, the government has eminent domain power to put a public road wherever it wants. As described in the next chapter, the compensation to which a property owner is entitled when land is taken for a public street is the difference between (1) the property's value in its highest and best use without the street and (2) such value with it. A rule requiring public control as a condition to a finding of a public prescriptive easement arguably aligns with a property owner's reasonable expectations, because the public nature of the use is apparent and its existence should already be incorporated into the property's market value. That is, the owner suffers no measurable

---

which regulate the acquisition of land by adverse possession. We find no basis in our decisions for holding that the general public cannot acquire by prescription rights such as those claimed here.").

46. 122 N.C. App. 322, 325–26, 469 S.E.2d 571, 574–75 (1996).

47. 177 N.C. App. 1, 15, 627 S.E.2d 650, 660 (2006) (quoting Hemphill v. Bd. of Alderman, 212 N.C. 185, 188, 193 S.E. 153, 155 (1937)).

48. *Id.* at 15–16, 627 S.E.2d at 661.

49. *Id.* at 15, 627 S.E.2d at 661.

economic loss from a finding that the street already exists. On the other hand, when the government has not shown sufficient interest in the road to exercise control over it or maintain it, its existence is less likely to have been incorporated into the valuation of the owner's land, which in turn strengthens the owner's claim to compensation. In such a case, if the government does not choose to acquire the public rights through eminent domain with payment of required compensation, individual neighbors who may have relied on the right of way over time are left to a claim that they have their own appurtenant prescriptive rights based on their specific history of use.

3.4 Neighborhood Roads

In 1931, the North Carolina General Assembly shifted control of county roads to the state Department of Transportation, which formerly was known as the State Highway Commission.[50] The General Assembly also provided, via statute, for continued public use of roads that the state did not carry over into its road system. With this statutory authority, any "interested party" may bring a special proceeding in superior court to establish the existence of a continuing easement as a "neighborhood public road" without future state highway control or maintenance.[51] This provision could be relevant to rights of way that were once outside municipal boundaries but that have since been incorporated within them, as well as to landowners interested in sources of rights to old roads that extend beyond municipal boundaries.

The statute provides for three kinds of neighborhood public roads. The first is "those portions of the public road system of the State which have not been taken over and placed under maintenance or which have been abandoned by the Department of Transportation, but which remain open and in general use as a necessary means of ingress to and egress from the dwelling house of one or more families."[52] As the North Carolina Court of Appeals instructed, "Whether a road constitutes a neighborhood public road must be determined as of the enactment date of the applicable statutory definition."[53] This definition of "neighborhood public road" was enacted in 1933.[54]

---

50. 1931 N.C. Sess. Laws ch. 145; Speight v. Anderson, 226 N.C. 492, 495, 39 S.E.2d 371, 373 (1946).

51. Chapter 136, Section 67 of the North Carolina General Statutes (hereinafter G.S.).

52. *Id.*

53. Roten v. Critcher, 135 N.C. App. 469, 473, 521 S.E.2d 140, 143 (1999).

54. 1933 N.C. Sess. Laws ch. 302; *Speight*, 226 N.C. at 495, 39 S.E.2d at 373.

A second type of right of way that can be declared a neighborhood public road is one that was "laid out, constructed, or reconstructed with unemployment relief funds under the supervision of the Department of Health and Human Services [(then the Department of Public Welfare)]."[55] This also was part of the 1933 legislation referenced above. New roads qualifying as such relief fund infrastructure are unlikely to be discovered today.

In 1941, the statute was amended to add a third type of neighborhood public road, which is "all other roads or streets or portions of roads or streets whatsoever outside of the boundaries of any incorporated city or town in the State which serve a public use regardless of whether the same have ever been a portion of any state or county road systems."[56] The 1941 change also added to the statute this qualification: "Provided, that this definition of neighborhood public roads shall not be construed to embrace any street, road or driveway that serves an essentially private use."[57] The North Carolina Court of Appeals instructed that for a right of way to qualify as such a road outside municipal boundaries, "regardless of whether the same have ever been a portion of any State or county road system," a claimant must prove that the right of way was "established by law by such means as dedication, condemnation or prescription" as of 1941.[58] Accordingly, if a road is alleged to have been created by public prescriptive use, that use would have to have begun no later than 1921 to meet the twenty-year occupancy requirement.[59]

In *Roten v. Critcher*, the North Carolina Court of Appeals held that the requirements of the neighborhood public roads statute were not met in that case because the claimant had obtained a right of use in a cartway proceeding that interrupted the required twenty years of continuous, prescriptive use.[60] As the North Carolina Supreme Court had earlier explained, "The General Assembly is without authority to create a public or private way over the lands of any citizen by legislative fiat, for, to do so, would be taking private property without just compensation."[61] As the court further explained: "It follows that the [1941 provision] necessarily refers to traveled ways which were at the time established easements or roads or streets in a legal sense. It cannot be construed to include ways of ingress and egress existing by consent of the landowner as a courtesy to a neighbor, nor to those adversely used for a time insufficient to create an easement."[62]

---

55. G.S. 136-67.
56. 1941 N.C. Sess. Laws ch. 183.
57. *Id.*
58. Roten v. Critcher, 135 N.C. App. 469, 473–74, 521 S.E.2d 140, 143–44 (1999).
59. *Id.*
60. *Id.* at 475, 521 S.E.2d at 144–45.
61. Speight v. Anderson, 226 N.C. 492, 496, 39 S.E.2d 371, 373 (1946).
62. *Id.*

As noted above, a right of way cannot qualify as a neighborhood public road under the statute if it "serves an essentially private use." The North Carolina Court of Appeals held that this exclusion applies to all three types of public roads. In other words, a road cannot qualify as a neighborhood public road if it was in essentially private use in 1941.[63] Accordingly, the statute was held not to apply to a right of way "used only as a private driveway for residents on land abutting the roadway . . . , even though guests and invitees of the residents also use it."[64]

The North Carolina Court of Appeals has explained that the "portions of roads" to which the first sentence of the neighborhood public roads statute refers means all of a road that was open and in general use as of the date the statute was enacted, including any portions of that road that might later be left unattended.[65]

---

63. Jarvis v. Powers, 80 N.C. App. 355, 366, 343 S.E.2d 195, 202 (1986).
64. *Id.* at 366, 343 S.E.2d at 201.
65. *Id.* at 363–64, 343 S.E.2d at 200–01.

4

Acquisition by Eminent Domain

American law has always sustained the power of federal, state, and local governments to use eminent domain to take property for use as a public road provided just compensation is paid to the owner for what is taken. North Carolina statutes authorize municipalities to use eminent domain to acquire property for roads and utilities, and they prescribe the procedure for accomplishing the acquisition and paying the required just compensation.

4.1 Municipal Eminent Domain Power

Chapter 160A, Section 240.1 of the North Carolina General Statutes (hereinafter G.S.) provides as follows: "A city may acquire, by gift, grant, devise, bequest, exchange, purchase, lease, or any other lawful method, the fee or any lesser interest in real or personal property for use by the city or any department, board, commission or agency of the city. In exercising the power of eminent domain a city shall use the procedures of [G.S.] Chapter 40A." Most purposes for which municipalities may exercise the eminent domain power are listed in G.S. 40A-3. Other statutes confirm municipal eminent domain powers for other particular purposes. Authorized municipal use of eminent domain power includes the following purposes:

- opening, widening, extending, or improving roads, streets, alleys, and sidewalks;[1]
- off-street parking facilities and systems;[2]
- public transportation systems;[3]
- establishing, extending, enlarging, or improving storm sewer and drainage systems and works or sewer and septic tank lines and systems, and drainage programs;[4]
- water supply and distribution systems;[5]

---

1. G.S. 40A-3(b)(1).
2. G.S. 40A-3(b)(2); 160A-311(8).
3. G.S. 40A-3(b)(2); 160A-311(5).
4. G.S. 40A-3(b)(4), (7).
5. G.S. 40A-3(b)(2); 160A-311(2).

- electric power generation, transmission, and distribution systems;[6]
- gas production, storage, transmission, and distribution systems, where work on systems also includes the purchase or lease of natural gas fields and natural gas reserves, the purchase of natural gas supplies, and the surveying, drilling, and any other activity related to the exploration for natural gas, whether in or outside the state;[7]
- cable television systems;[8]
- stormwater management programs;[9] and
- airports.[10]

Local acts authorize certain municipalities to use the procedures available to the North Carolina Department of Transportation in G.S. Chapter 136, Article 9 for specific purposes, including, for example, streets and highways, public transportation, water and sewer systems, and other infrastructure.[11]

G.S. Chapter 162A gives eminent domain power to other local government organizations that provide water or sewer systems, which can mean a single political subdivision or a consortium of more than one. The organizations granted the power of eminent domain include water and sewer system authorities, metropolitan water districts, and metropolitan sewer districts. Sanitary district boards, which may also perform water and sewer functions, also have eminent domain power. Certain beach communities have eminent domain power to acquire public trust beaches and appurtenant parking areas, as well as wharves.[12]

The courts have held that an authority with eminent domain power has discretion to choose the property to be taken if the purpose is legislatively authorized and constitutionally permissible. As described in section 1.1, *supra*, North Carolina's courts presume that public officials act legally and in good faith when making choices about public projects. This discretion includes the scope and location of a given project and extends to the determination of the extent of the interest to be acquired in the needed property, whether it should be ownership in fee or a limited easement right.[13] For example, courts will not scrutinize a decision to widen a street without a showing of bad faith or obvious abuse of discretion.[14] As the North

---

6. G.S. 40A-3(b)(2); 160A-311(1).

7. G.S. 40A-3(b)(2); 160A-311(4).

8. G.S. 40A-3(b)(2); 160A-311(7).

9. G.S. 40A-3(b)(2); 160A-311(10).

10. G.S. 40A-3(b)(2); 160A-311(9).

11. *E.g.,* S.L. 2001-304 (Charlotte, for stormwater and public transportation); S.L. 2000-89 (Charlotte, for economic development).

12. G.S. 40A-3(b1).

13. City of Charlotte v. Cook, 348 N.C. 222, 225–27, 498 S.E.2d 605, 607–09 (1998).

14. City of Charlotte v. McNeely, 281 N.C. 684, 690, 190 S.E.2d 179, 184–85 (1972).

Carolina Court of Appeals explained, "Even where less intrusive means of accomplishing the public purpose exist, a condemnation will not be invalidated when the taking is not arbitrary and capricious and is necessary to accomplish the purpose."[15]

Notwithstanding the broad discretion afforded local governments to determine the property needed for a public project, G.S. Chapter 40A contains certain express constraints regarding a local government's use of eminent domain for the acquisition of an entire parcel or building when the intended use only requires a portion of that parcel or building. The relevant statute in this chapter provides, "When the proposed project requires condemnation of only a portion of a parcel of land leaving a remainder of such shape, size or condition that it is of little value, a condemnor may acquire the entire parcel by purchase or condemnation."[16] The condemnor has the threshold burden of establishing that the remainder is "of little value."[17] In addition to meeting this burden, the condemnor must allege in the complaint, and be prepared to establish, that one of the following conditions exists: "a partial taking of the land would substantially destroy the economic value or utility of the remainder," "an economy in the expenditure of public funds will be promoted by taking the entire parcel," or "the interest of the public will be best served by acquiring the entire parcel."[18] When the eminent domain acquisition involves a portion of a building, the complaint must recite that the condemnor has determined that "an economy in the expenditure of public funds will be promoted by acquiring the entire building or structure," "it is not feasible to cut off a portion of the building or structure without destroying the whole," or "the convenience, safety, or improvement of the project will be promoted by acquiring the entire building or structure."[19] The condemnor is not required to integrate the remainder of the land or building acquired into the project and is free to sell or exchange it for other property.

---

15. Transcontinental Gas Pipe Line Corp. v. Calco Enters., 132 N.C. App. 237, 245, 511 S.E.2d 671, 677 (1999).

16. G.S. 40A-7(a).

17. Piedmont Triad Reg'l Water Auth. v. Sumner Hills Inc., 353 N.C. 343, 346–47, 543 S.E.2d 844, 847 (2001).

18. G.S. 40A-7(a); *see Piedmont Triad Reg'l Water Auth.*, 353 N.C. at 347, 543 S.E.2d at 847–48 (condemnor has burden of affirmatively establishing that the proposed condemnation of remaining property is authorized because it meets one of the conditions in G.S. 40A-7(a)).

19. G.S. 40A-7(c).

4.2 Compensation

When property is taken by eminent domain, the federal and state constitutions require that "just compensation" be paid to the owner of the property.[20] Just compensation is fair market value based on the acquired property's potential "highest and best use," not just its current use or its currently contemplated use. As the North Carolina Supreme Court explained: "In determining the value of land appropriated for public purposes, the same considerations are to be regarded as in a sale of property between private parties. The inquiry in such cases must be, What is the property worth in the market, viewed not merely with reference to the uses to which it is plainly adapted; that is to say, what is it worth from its availability for valuable uses?"[21] For municipal takings, the statutes specify that "[t]he determination of the amount of compensation shall reflect the value of the property immediately prior to the filing of [a petition for appraisal by the property owner or the filing of a complaint by the public condemnor declaring the taking of the property] and except as provided in the following sections shall not reflect an increase or decrease due to the condemnation. The day of the filing of a petition or complaint shall be the date of valuation of the interest taken."[22]

Accordingly, a parcel's capacity for subdivision and development is a factor to be considered when determining its market value. Appraisers take parcel size and physical characteristics into account to determine what a potential purchaser would pay. One detail to be weighed in this analysis is the likelihood of obtaining required local land use approvals for the proposed property development. If approvals are unlikely because of the property's characteristics, the value appropriately would be less than if the approvals had been obtained. The North Carolina Court of Appeals has said, "If an owner has taken steps prior to the date of taking to adapt his land for future uses, the future uses to which the land is adapted are admissible."[23] For example, if a development plat has received regulatory approvals and roads have been installed, the lots likely would be valued as subdivided lots.[24] On the other hand, valuations based on speculative uses, or on unreasonable optimism about regulatory approvals, would likely not be considered.

The usual approach to determining fair market value for residential properties is "market comparison." Appraisers identify neighborhoods with properties similar to the subject parcel, research recent sales information, and make adjustments for

---

20. U.S. Const. amend. V; N.C. Const. art. I, § 19.

21. Carolina-Tenn. Power Co. v. Hiawassee River Power Co., 186 N.C. 179, 183–84, 119 S.E. 213, 215 (1923) (quoting Boom Co. v. Patterson, 98 U.S. 403, 407–08 (1878)).

22. G.S. 40A-63.

23. City of Wilson v. Hawley, 156 N.C. App. 609, 613, 577 S.E.2d 161, 164 (2003).

24. Town of Hillsborough v. Crabtree, 143 N.C. App. 707, 710, 547 S.E.2d 139, 141 (2001).

differences in lot and building size and other characteristics.[25] For some types of property, the "income approach" may be appropriate. This approach reflects the reality that income-producing property, such as a shopping center or apartment building, is purchased for investment, and the amount a purchaser will pay reflects anticipated returns based on the property's characteristics and the market for them. The appraiser using an income approach calculates anticipated income using information about market rents, vacancy rates, maintenance and operating costs, and sometimes other factors, and then converts the anticipated income stream to a value using an "income rate" or "discount rate" intended to reflect the present value of the anticipated income stream.[26] In rare circumstances, a third measure, the cost approach, is used. The North Carolina Supreme Court instructed that "the cost approach involves a determination of the fair market value of the (vacant) land, the cost of reproduction of the buildings or replacement thereof by new buildings of modern design and materials less depreciation."[27] The cost approach generally is not used when sufficient data are available for developing a valuation using the market comparison or income approach. It may be viewed as the best method for a unique property for which there is insufficient market information about comparable properties.

The general rule applied by the courts, subject to limited exceptions involving unusual use of eminent domain, "is that loss of profits from the operation of a business conducted on the property is not an element of recoverable damages in an award pursuant to an eminent domain taking."[28] The statutes governing local government eminent domain also do not include business relocation expenses as part of the required compensation to the property owner, and the courts have held that such expenses are not recoverable in the absence of a statutory requirement or agreement.[29] The distinction between diminished real estate value, for which an owner must be compensated, and lost business profits, which have been held not to be compensable, can be difficult to discern. As stated above, the income approach to valuing commercial real estate involves calculating expected income from the real estate based on market rents, vacancy rates, and maintenance and operating costs. On the other hand, the courts have made clear that both the federal and state constitutions require payment for the real estate taken, not for anticipated lost profits from a going-concern business.[30] The North Carolina Supreme Court

---

25. Redev. Comm'n of High Point v. Denny Roll & Panel Co., 273 N.C. 368, 371, 159 S.E.2d 863, 863 (1968).

26. Dep't of Transp. v. Fleming, 112 N.C. App. 580, 583, 436 S.E.2d 407, 409 (1993).

27. *Redev. Comm'n of High Point*, 273 N.C. at 370–71, 159 S.E.2d at 863.

28. *Fleming*, 112 N.C. App. at 582, 436 S.E.2d at 409.

29. Williams v. State Highway Comm'n, 252 N.C. 141, 145, 113 S.E.2d 263, 267 (1960).

30. Dep't of Transp. v. M.M. Fowler, Inc., 361 N.C. 1, 12–15, 637 S.E.2d 885, 894–95 (2006).

explained that "with the income approach, the appraisal must differentiate between income directly from the property and profits of the business located on the land."[31]

In the typical case of a street widening, a municipality will only take a strip of property for the expansion rather than an entire lot. Often the value of this strip is only a portion of the overall raw land value, but in any particular case the economic impact can be significant, such as when the taking makes the property inaccessible. The statute that applies when a local government acquires part of a tract provides that the amount of compensation is the greater of the figures resulting from two measures.[32] The first measure is "the amount by which the fair market value of the entire tract immediately before the taking exceeds the fair market value of the remainder immediately after the taking."[33] The second measure is "the fair market value of the property taken."[34] Consequently, if the rights taken do not appreciably diminish the remainder's value, the owner can recover an amount equal to the value of the property taken.

The statutes provide that three circumstances should not be considered in a valuation for eminent domain compensation. First, the valuation should not be affected by any change before the date of valuation caused by "the proposed improvement or project for which the property is taken."[35] In other words, the valuation is of the property's highest and best use—as if the property were not under a "cloud" of condemnation or the promise of it.[36] Second, the valuation should not be affected by "the reasonable likelihood that the property would be acquired for [the subject] improvement or project."[37] Third, the valuation should not be affected by "the condemnation proceeding in which the property is taken."[38] The North Carolina Court of Appeals has described these rules as "intended to level the playing field and ensure that neither party receives a windfall as a result of the condemnation."[39]

Property that is taken by eminent domain often is subject to a lender's security interest. Loan agreements between property owners and lenders typically specify how eminent domain proceedings affect the status of the security interest and the parties' relative rights to condemnation awards. Deeds of trust typically provide

---

31. *Id.* at 13, 637 S.E.2d at 894.

32. G.S. 40A-64(b).

33. G.S. 40A-64(b)(i).

34. G.S. 40A-64(b)(ii).

35. G.S. 40A-65(a)(i).

36. Raleigh-Durham Airport Auth. v. King, 75 N.C. App. 57, 61–62, 330 S.E.2d 622, 625 (1985).

37. G.S. 40A-65(a)(ii).

38. G.S. 40A-65(a)(iii).

39. Piedmont Triad Reg'l Water Auth. v. Unger, 154 N.C. App. 589, 593, 572 S.E.2d 832, 835 (2002).

that the lender is entitled to receive condemnation proceeds and apply them to the secured debt. If an entire parcel is taken, the secured lender will want to apply the proceeds to payment of the secured debt. Secured lenders often assert a right to the proceeds even if only part of the secured premises is taken, or if limited rights, such as easements, are acquired by eminent domain. The statutes governing municipal exercise of eminent domain contain two provisions specifically affecting the relationship between the lender and the owner that expressly override any agreement between the parties. The first provides that in the case of a partial taking, "the lienholder may share in the amount of compensation awarded only to the extent determined by the commissioners [of appraisal] or by the jury [if the compensation amount was appealed] or by the judge [in the condemnation proceeding] to be necessary to prevent an impairment of his security, and the lien shall continue upon the part of the property not taken as security for the unpaid portion of the indebtedness until it is paid."[40] The second provision invalidates prepayment penalties because of a condemnation, stating that "[n]either the condemnor nor owner is liable to the lienholder for any penalty for prepayment of the debt secured by the lien, and the amount awarded by the judgment to the lienholder shall not include any penalty therefor."[41]

When a temporary easement is taken, such as a construction easement used to move or store equipment on someone's land, the valuation might appropriately consider the fair rental value of the easement area during the time of use; the costs incurred by the property owner in removing or altering his or her improvements to accommodate the public project; the costs to the owner of alternative access; the value of removed trees, crops, or other improvements; and any resulting diminished value to the owner's remaining property.[42] As the North Carolina Court of Appeals summarized, for such circumstances the award is for "the rental value during the period of the taking, together with any damage sustained by the property."[43] The court explained that a damage award for a temporary construction easement "considers interference with the property's use *during* the construction, but not the impact of the project as completed on the remaining property's value as a whole."[44] Lost business profits are not compensable.[45]

---

40. G.S. 40A-68(1).
41. G.S. 40A-68(2).
42. Colonial Pipeline Co. v. Weaver, 310 N.C. 93, 107, 310 S.E.2d 338, 346 (1984).
43. City of Charlotte v. Combs, 216 N.C. App. 258, 262, 719 S.E.2d 59, 63 (2011) (quoting 26 Am. Jur. 2d *Eminent Domain* § 283).
44. Dep't of Transp. v. Jay Butmataji, LLC, 818 S.E.2d 171, 175 (N.C. Ct. App. 2018) (emphasis in original).
45. *Id.* at 177.

4.3 Eminent Domain Procedure

In the typical situation, a condemning authority will contact a property owner and attempt to reach an agreement for the purchase of what is needed for street construction or expansion before commencing any eminent domain litigation. Typically, an appraisal will have been done that can be shared with the owner to show the fairness of the amount offered. A municipality is not required to make an offer of compensation before filing an eminent domain action,[46] but if one is made, it will not be admissible evidence of the property's value if a condemnation proceeding becomes necessary.[47]

A municipality that seeks to purchase property, or to acquire it by gift, must give written notice to the owner of the owner's right to reimbursement of the pro rata portion of paid real estate taxes attributable to the period after title vests in the condemnor.[48] "Natural persons" who own land taken by eminent domain, who also own adjacent agricultural land, horticultural land, or forestland, may also be entitled to notice of a right to reimbursement of deferred taxes.[49]

A municipality intending to use eminent domain is authorized by statute to enter "any lands" to conduct investigations "as may be necessary or expedient in carrying out and performing its rights or duties" in connection with the eminent domain action, for the purpose of surveying, examining, or conducting tests, including borings.[50] The statutes require at least thirty days' prior written notice to the owners and parties in possession before going onto the land.[51]

At least thirty days before a municipality files an eminent domain case, the municipality must mail to the property owner a notice of action, with statutorily required information, including a description of the property and the estimated amount of compensation.[52]

An eminent domain action is commenced with the filing in superior court of (1) a complaint containing a declaration of taking and (2) an attached notice of deposit reflecting "the sum of money estimated by the condemnor to be just compensation for the taking."[53] Among other things, the condemnor must in the complaint or in an attachment to it identify or describe the following: all of the owners having an interest in the subject property; the existence of liens or other

---

46. G.S. 40A-4.
47. Barnes v. N.C. State Highway Comm'n, 250 N.C. 378, 396, 109 S.E.2d 219, 233 (1959).
48. G.S. 40A-4; 40A-6.
49. G.S. 40A-6(b).
50. G.S. 40A-11.
51. *Id.*
52. G.S. 40A-40.
53. G.S. 40A-41.

encumbrances that can be ascertained; the property to be acquired and any other property affected, such as remaining property after part of a tract is taken; whether the owner may remove improvements or fixtures; and notice that the required deposit has been made with the court.[54]

When a municipality files an eminent domain case, it must deposit, "to the use of the owner," the estimated amount of just compensation.[55] The owner may withdraw this amount without losing the ability to prove entitlement to more.[56] Most eminent domain cases are only about the amount of just compensation, because, in view of the discretion that municipalities have regarding the location and scope of public projects, there rarely is any sound basis to challenge the authority for the taking.

A condemnor filing an eminent domain complaint must at the time of filing record a "memorandum of action" with the register of deeds in each county in which the land involved is located.[57] This notice is a means by which condemnors ensure that the outcome of an eminent domain proceeding will bind any party acquiring an interest in the property after the action has been commenced.

The condemnor must serve the summons, along with a copy of the complaint and notice of deposit, in the manner prescribed by the North Carolina Rules of Civil Procedure.[58] However, property owners and other parties have an extended period of 120 days from the date of service to file an answer.[59] With an answer, an owner responds to the condemnor's allegations, makes any affirmative claims, and may demand that a jury decide the amount of just compensation. The condemnor then has ninety days to file a reply, which is an optional response to the owner's answer.[60]

Within ninety days from receipt of the answer, but no sooner than six months after the complaint is filed, the condemnor must file with the superior court "a plat of the property taken and such additional area as may be necessary to determine the compensation"; a copy of the plat must be mailed to the parties to the action or to their attorneys.[61]

After an eminent domain action has begun, the parties will exchange information about their claims and positions, including information about how they value the property being acquired. The parties may be able to reach an agreement on the amount of compensation at any time during an eminent domain proceeding.

---

54. *Id.*
55. *Id.*
56. G.S. 40A-44.
57. G.S. 40A-43.
58. G.S. 40A-41; 1A-1, Rule 4.
59. G.S. 40A-46.
60. G.S. 40A-45(a); 40A-46.
61. G.S. 40A-45(c).

At the trial on the matter, the court will decide legal issues, including disputes about what property is being taken, the proper parties to the action, or competing claims to the deposit.[62] The issue of just compensation will be submitted to a jury if a jury trial was demanded by either party, or the parties can elect to have the issue decided by three appointed commissioners or by a judge.[63]

After all the issues have been decided, final judgment will be entered, which will be filed with the register of deeds to reflect the transfer of ownership. The condemnor will pay to the property owner any amounts still owed for just compensation to the extent not already paid by withdrawal from the deposit.

The law enables governments to move forward with most public projects without having to wait for a final resolution of disputes about how much compensation must be paid to affected property owners. Under North Carolina law, most acquisitions are made by a "quick-take" procedure, by which the government acquires title and the right to possession of the subject property as soon as the government files a complaint, a declaration of taking, and a deposit of estimated compensation with the court. The quick-take procedure applies to municipal acquisitions for roads, sidewalks, and utilities,[64] but it does not apply to public transportation systems, off-street parking facilities, airports, or stormwater management programs. If the government is taking property for purposes to which the quick-take procedure does not apply, in most cases the title will vest in the government when the owner files an answer.

Sometimes owners believe that their property has been taken without the government having followed the eminent domain procedure and paying compensation. When the government occupies or uses someone's property under circumstances in which compensation must be paid, without first following the eminent domain procedure, the owner may have a claim for what is referred to as "inverse condemnation." A landowner in this situation may file an action against a municipality that takes property for street or utility purposes without having followed an eminent domain proceedure.[65] G.S. 40A-51 provides that "[t]he action may be initiated within 24 months of the date of the taking of the affected property or the completion of the project involving the taking, whichever shall occur later." This limitation period applies regardless of whether the condemnor intended to include in its taking the property alleged to have been taken without an eminent domain proceeding.[66] If a public project has discrete subparts, the limitations period will

---

62. G.S. 40A-47.
63. G.S. 1A-1, Rule 38; 40A-48.
64. G.S. 40A-42(a)(1).
65. G.S. 40A-51(a).
66. Wilcox v. N.C. State Highway Comm'n, 279 N.C. 185, 187-88, 181 S.E.2d 435, 437 (1971).

be measured from the date on which the effects of the subparts become apparent, rather than from when the overall project is commenced. In *McAdoo v. City of Greensboro*,[67] a road-widening project was completed in sections, with different contractors performing the work on individual sections. The North Carolina Court of Appeals, construing a statute of limitations period that began to run upon "the completion of the project" involving the taking, held that each section could be deemed a "project."[68]

The limitations period for filing a claim for physical damage to property as a result of eminent domain is specified in G.S. 1-52(16), which requires that the action be filed within three years after the physical damage "becomes apparent or ought reasonably to have become apparent to the claimant," whichever occurs first, but no later than ten years after the last act or omission on which the claim is based.[69]

4.4 Statutory Right to Cartways

The North Carolina General Statutes provide an unusual procedure that enables a private landowner to use the eminent domain superior court process discussed in section 4.3, *supra*, to establish an open right of way at least eighteen feet wide over someone else's property for access to a public road if no private route is available.[70] The right of way—referred to in the statutes as a *cartway*—must be needed for certain productive uses or church access, and compensation must be paid for any diminution in value to the landowner. A petition for a cartway is most likely to arise today in connection with timber harvesting, which may involve the kind of land that tends not to have ready road access.[71]

Essentially, the cartway procedure set out in G.S. 136-69 is a means for an individual landowner to connect to the highway system without government expense. It has been statutorily authorized since 1798.[72] The North Carolina Supreme Court said that cartways established through this statutory procedure "are public roads in

---

67. 91 N.C. App. 570, 372 S.E.2d 742 (1988).

68. *Id.* at 572–73, 372 S.E.2d at 744 (construing G.S. 40A-51(a)).

69. *See* Robertson v. City of High Point, 129 N.C. App. 88, 91, 497 S.E.2d 300, 302 (1998) (discussing statutes of limitation).

70. G.S. 136-69.

71. *E.g.*, Greene v. Garner, 163 N.C. App. 142, 592 S.E.2d 589 (2004) (tract divided by Interstate 95 without means of access to that highway).

72. *See generally* Joseph J. Kalo & Monica Kivel Kalo, *Putting the Cartway Before the House: Statutory Easements by Necessity, or Cartways, in North Carolina*, 75 N.C. L. Rev. 1943, 1947–48 (1977).

the sense that they are open to all who see fit to use them" and that the reference to a "private way" in the statute merely distinguishes who bears the cost—the landowner who brought the action, rather than the public.[73] Accordingly, if a cartway is established, its use is not limited to the person or entity who brought the procedure and paid compensation as part of it. The North Carolina Supreme Court explained that "although established and opened upon the petition of private landowners, and primarily for their benefit, [cartways] are, as provided by our statute, open for the free passage of all persons on horse, foot, in wagons or carts. This extension of their use impresses upon them a public character. In this way the power to invoke the right of eminent domain for the purpose of opening and maintaining them, is sustained."[74] In other words, the cartway's interconnectedness with the highway system is an essential element to satisfy the public purpose or benefit requirement for constitutionally permissible takings.[75]

According to the North Carolina Court of Appeals' distillation of the statute, three elements must be satisfied to establish a cartway: "1) the land in question is used for one of the purposes enumerated in the statute; 2) the land is without adequate access to a public road or other adequate means of transportation affording necessary and proper ingress and egress; and, 3) the granting of a private way over the lands of *other persons* is necessary, reasonable and just."[76]

To satisfy the authorized purpose requirement in the cartway procedure, a person or entity must be "engaged in the cultivation of any land or the cutting and removing of any standing timber, or the working of any quarries, mines, or minerals, or the operating of any industrial or manufacturing plants, or public or private cemetery, or taking action preparatory to the operation of any such enterprises."[77] In addition, a North Carolina statute authorizes use of the procedure for "[n]ecessary roads or easements and right-of-ways for electric light lines, power lines, water lines, sewage lines, and telephone lines leading to any church or other place of public worship."[78]

The required authorized purpose need not be an exclusive one. The North Carolina Supreme Court interpreted G.S. 136-69 as "not limit[ing] the uses to those specified in the statute if in fact there are uses which do meet statutory

---

73. Parsons v. Wright, 223 N.C. 520, 521, 27 S.E.2d 534, 536–37 (1943).

74. Cozad v. Hardwood Co., 139 N.C. 283, 287–88, 51 S.E. 932, 934 (1905).

75. Carolina Tel. & Tel. Co. v. McLeod, 321 N.C. 426, 432–33, 364 S.E.2d 399, 402–03 (1988).

76. Greene v. Garner, 163 N.C. App. 142, 147, 592 S.E.2d 589, 592–93 (2004) (quoting Davis v. Forsyth Cty., 117 N.C. App. 725, 727, 453 S.E.2d 231, 232 (1995) (emphasis added by the court).

77. G.S. 136-69(a).

78. G.S. 136-71.

requirements."[79] The statute speaks of uses for which a cartway is needed in the present tense, but it also refers to "action preparatory to the operation of any such enterprises," and cartways have been established based on a convincing case for anticipated timber operations.[80] The North Carolina Supreme Court held that a petitioner's intent to use a small portion of a parcel of land for pasturing cattle and another portion for timbering were sufficient intended purposes and that the statutory remedy was not invalidated by an intent to also use the property for hunting.[81] On the other hand, the North Carolina Court of Appeals sustained a rejection of a cartway on the basis that the petitioner's timber harvesting intentions were not "legitimate" because he actually planned to use the subject site for dances and recreational activities.[82]

The statute also requires that the site be one "to which there is leading no public road or other adequate means of transportation, other than a navigable waterway, affording necessary and proper means of ingress thereto and egress therefrom."[83] A party cannot use the cartway procedure if there is access through another route, even by means of an easement that is not permanent. A sufficient alternative easement right need only be a "reasonable permissive right of way."[84]

Finally, for a cartway to be established the statute requires that the court conclude that the granting of a private way over the lands of other persons is "necessary, reasonable and just."[85] As the North Carolina Supreme Court explained: "This statutory provision is in derogation of the free and unrestricted use and enjoyment of the land by the owner thereof over which the cartway is established, and must be construed strictly. The petitioner is not entitled to have it simply as a convenience, or because it enables him to reach a public road, ferry, bridge, or public landing from the land upon which he may be settled, or which he may be cultivating, by a shorter or more convenient route, but because there is no public road serving such purpose, and because also it is 'necessary, reasonable and just' that he should have the cartway."[86]

By statute, the rights to a cartway terminate automatically after five years unless, when the cartway was established, a longer term was set. Cartway rights can also be for an indefinite term. For example, the state court of appeals approved a permanent cartway when the petitioner sought its use for a timber operation that took

79. Candler v. Sluder, 259 N.C. 62, 65, 130 S.E.2d 1, 4 (1963).
80. Greene v. Garner, 163 N.C. App. 142, 148, 592 S.E.2d 589, 593 (2004).
81. *Candler,* 259 N.C. at 65, 130 S.E.2d at 4.
82. Turlington v. McLeod, 79 N.C. App. 299, 305–06, 339 S.E.2d 44, 48–49 (1986).
83. G.S. 136-69(a).
84. *Turlington,* 79 N.C. App. at 305, 339 S.E.2d at 49.
85. *Greene,* 163 N.C. App. at 147, 592 S.E.2d at 592–93.
86. Warlick v. Lowman, 103 N.C. 122, 124, 9 S.E. 458, 459 (1889).

thirty to thirty-five years for harvesting and reforestation and the Forest Service said that immediately available access was necessary "to inspect the timber for infestation and storm damage."[87]

A petitioner must prove the statutory elements for a cartway in a special proceeding before the clerk of the superior court in the county where the subject property is situated.[88] When a petition for a cartway is filed, the court appoints "a jury of view of three disinterested freeholders to view the premises and lay off" a cartway at least eighteen feet wide.[89] "Once the right to a cartway has been determined, the mechanics of locating and laying it off is for the jury of view—it is for them to determine the location, its termini, and the land to be burdened thereby."[90] The clerk of superior court reviews the jury's report and may affirm or modify it or order a new jury of view.[91]

The owner whose property is subjected to a cartway is entitled to compensation as assessed in eminent domain,[92] as described in section 4.2, *supra*. Any interested party has a right of appeal to the superior court for a jury trial de novo on all issues related to the cartway determination, including compensation.[93]

G.S. 136-69 allows establishment of a cartway on government land if the requisite conditions can be shown.[94]

---

87. *Greene*, 163 N.C. App. at 148–49, 592 S.E.2d at 593.
88. G.S. 136-68.
89. G.S. 136-69(a).
90. Candler v. Sluder, 259 N.C. 62, 67, 130 S.E.2d 1, 5 (1963).
91. G.S. 136-69(a).
92. G.S. 136-69(b).
93. Greene v. Garner, 163 N.C. App. 142, 145–46, 592 S.E.2d 589, 591–92 (2004).
94. Davis v. Forsyth Cty., 117 N.C. App. 725, 727, 453 S.E.2d 231, 232 (1995).

5

Street Access and Maintenance

A municipal government's responsibility for its public streets falls into two general categories: what is owed to abutters who own lots that share a boundary with a street for their rights of access and what is owed to the public generally for keeping streets open and free from negligently created, dangerous conditions.

5.1 Restrictions on Abutter Entry and Exit

A municipality cannot eliminate all forms of access from an abutting lot to a public street without compensating the lot owner for the loss.[1] The North Carolina Supreme Court held that a taking occurred when a right of access to an abutting highway was cut off, even though the lot continued to have direct access to two other public streets.[2] The court said that "where all direct access to a highway has been eliminated or substantially interfered with, causing diminution in value of an abutting property, the landowner is entitled to damages therefor."[3] As described in the next chapter, state laws protect an abutter who depends entirely on a street by allowing its permanent closure only if "no individual owning property in the vicinity of the street or alley or in the subdivision in which it is located would thereby be deprived of reasonable means of ingress and egress to his property."[4] Accordingly, today a municipality is most likely to encounter claims regarding rights of access when it makes changes that make it more difficult to get to or from an abutter's premises, rather than a change that entirely isolates an abutter from the street system.

Abutter access may be affected when a municipality widens a street. When a portion of private property is needed for the added width, the municipality likely will reach an agreement with the owner for purchase of the required public easement in a manner that leaves the owner with adequate direct access to the newly configured street. If no agreement can be reached, the municipality has the power to take the needed land by eminent domain, in which case the municipality must

---

1. Dep't of Transp. v. Harkey, 308 N.C. 148, 158, 301 S.E.2d 64, 71 (1983).
2. *Id.*
3. *Id.* at 154, 301 S.E.2d at 68.
4. Chapter 160A, Section 299(a) of the North Carolina General Statutes (hereinafter G.S.).

pay for the diminished value of the affected land. A disputed claim to compensation is more likely to arise with a street project for which no provision is made for owner agreement or payment, such as a re-routing that changes the flow of traffic.

The basis for an abutter's claim to compensation for a street reconfiguration is the right to use a street on which a lot abuts. As the North Carolina Supreme Court said, "It is generally recognized that the owner of land abutting a highway has a right beyond that which is enjoyed by the general public, a special right of easement in the public road for access purposes, and this is a property right which cannot be damaged or taken from him without due compensation."[5] As the court further explained, "But a landowner is not entitled, as against the public, to access to his land at all points in the boundary between it and the highway, although entire access cannot be cut off. If he has free and convenient access to his property, and his means of ingress and egress are not substantially interfered with by the public, he has no cause of complaint."[6]

Accordingly, a municipality has the power to regulate points of access as long as an affected lot is left with the reasonable possibility of legal use of the public street. A municipality may limit the number of points of vehicular access to a street and regulate their location[7] and may also require that an existing point of access be relocated.[8] Installation of traffic medians,[9] removal of sidewalks,[10] and designation of one-way streets have become well-settled, permissible regulations.[11] For instance, the North Carolina Supreme Court held that the installation of islands that channeled access to a commercial site was reasonable and did not substantially interfere with access such that compensation was required.[12] It also held that no taking occurs if the subject property is connected to the highway at issue by means of a service road.[13] Such restrictions may be undertaken pursuant to the government unit's police power, and in "the interest of public safety, convenience and general welfare,"[14] without triggering any obligation to pay compensation.

---

5. Abdalla v. State Highway Comm'n, 261 N.C. 114, 118, 134 S.E.2d 81, 84 (1964).

6. Barnes v. N.C. State Highway Comm'n, 257 N.C. 507, 517, 126 S.E.2d 732, 739 (1962) (quoting 39 C.J.S. *Highways* § 141).

7. *Abdalla*, 261 N.C. at 118–20, 134 S.E.2d at 84–85.

8. Haymore v. N.C. State Highway Comm'n, 14 N.C. App. 691, 694–96, 189 S.E.2d 611, 613–14 (1972).

9. Gene's, Inc. v. City of Charlotte, 259 N.C. 118, 121, 129 S.E.2d 889, 891–92 (1963).

10. Crotts v. City of Winston-Salem, 170 N.C. 24, 27–28, 86 S.E. 792, 794 (1915).

11. *Barnes*, 257 N.C. at 517–18, 126 S.E.2d at 740–41.

12. State Highway Comm'n v. Rose, 31 N.C. App. 28, 32–33, 228 S.E.2d 664, 664–66 (1976).

13. N.C. State Highway Comm'n v. Nuckles, 271 N.C. 1, 19–22, 155 S.E.2d 772, 787–89 (1967).

14. Snow v. N.C. State Highway Comm'n, 262 N.C. 169, 175, 136 S.E.2d 678, 683 (1964).

Changes in general traffic flow also are unlikely to trigger a right to compensation. Explaining the rule, the North Carolina Supreme Court quoted the following language from a Washington state case in which a landowner claimed that a taking occurred after the state installed a median that required drivers in one direction of travel to take a different route to reach the landowners' commercial property:

> Plaintiffs have no property right in the continuation or maintenance of the flow of traffic past their property. They still have free and unhampered ingress and egress to their property. Once on the Highway, to which they have free access, they are in the same position as every other member of the traveling public. Plaintiffs, and every member of the traveling public subject to traffic regulations, have the same right of free access *to* the property *from* the highway. Re-routing and diversion of traffic are police power regulations. Circuity of route, resulting from an exercise of the police power, is an incidental result of a lawful act. It is not the taking or damaging of a property right.[15]

As the North Carolina Supreme Court further explained in a later case, "To entitle a landowner to damages in the closing of a portion of a highway, he must show that he has suffered an injury different in kind from that suffered by the general public."[16] Consequently, the court held that an owner is not entitled to compensation merely because some of the passing traffic has been diminished by a change in configuration, because nearly every owner would be entitled to compensation whenever improvements were made to reduce hazards.[17]

In some circumstances, however, the effect of changes in a road's configuration can actually render abutting property nearly worthless if the changes make any access impossible or unreasonably difficult. In an early case, *Harper v. Town of Lenoir*,[18] the North Carolina Supreme Court affirmed an award of damages when grade changes resulted in a ledge that separated the owner's land from the road at issue. More recently, the North Carolina Court of Appeals explained that "a property owner is entitled to compensation as a matter of law, even if direct access to the abutting road is not completely eliminated, but is substantially interfered with by the State. To determine if the defendant's direct access to the abutting road

---

15. *Barnes*, 257 N.C. at 516, 126 S.E.2d at 738–39 (emphasis added by the court) (quoting Walker v. State of Washington, 295 P.2d 328, 331 (Wash. 1956)).
16. *Snow*, 262 N.C. at 173, 136 S.E.2d at 682.
17. *Id.* at 174, 136 S.E.2d at 682.
18. 152 N.C. 723, 68 S.E. 228 (1910).

has been substantially interfered with, the trial court must determine whether a 'reasonable means of ingress and egress remains or is provided.'"[19]

The availability and nature of alternate access routes therefore are key factors that courts consider when determining whether road changes have the kind of impact that requires compensation for economic loss. The North Carolina Supreme Court has instructed that compensation will be appropriate "where all direct access to a highway has been eliminated or substantially interfered with, causing diminution in value of an abutting property."[20] In *Department of Transportation v. Harkey*,[21] the affected landowner, which used the subject property for a church, sought damages when the state converted a road fronting the property into a controlled-access highway, which left the affected lot with frontage on two other local roads running along other sides of the lot. The connection to the new controlled-access highway—which used to be a frontage road with direct access to the lot—required navigation "via various paved streets in what is generally a residential area."[22] The court said that under "established precedent"—as well as a state statute governing state controlled-access highways—the relegation to indirect access across local traffic lanes was a taking and that the state must pay for any diminution in value it caused.[23] Under such circumstances, compensation owed, if any, is based on the diminished value of the affected tract.[24]

5.2 Grade Changes

Changes in street grade can seriously affect an abutter's access to a public street because of the resulting unevenness in elevation between the street and the abutter's lot. The long-standing rule in North Carolina is that no taking occurs when a non-negligent change of grade is made in a street.[25] The courts' disinclination to see a need for compensation for a grade change emerged from early cases in which storefront property owners sought compensation after sidewalks were changed

---

19. Dep't of Transp. v. BB&R, LLC, 242 N.C. App. 11, 17, 775 S.E.2d 8, 13–14 (2015) (quoting State Highway Comm'n v. Yarborough, 6 N.C. App. 294, 302, 170 S.E.2d 159, 165 (1969)).

20. Dep't of Transp. v. Harkey, 308 N.C. 148, 154, 301 S.E.2d 64, 68 (1983).

21. 308 N.C. 148, 301 S.E.2d 64 (1983).

22. *Id.* at 150, 301 S.E.2d at 66.

23. *Id.* at 158–59, 301 S.E.2d at 70–71.

24. Dr. T.C. Smith Co. v. N.C. State Highway Comm'n, 279 N.C. 328, 335, 182 S.E.2d 383, 387 (1971).

25. Smith v. State Highway Comm'n, 257 N.C. 410, 126 S.E.2d 87 (1962); Dorsey v. Town of Henderson, 148 N.C. 423, 62 S.E. 547 (1908).

and the owners needed to install steps or other accommodations.[26] The North Carolina Supreme Court emphasized, however, that the street work must be done "with ordinary skill and caution" and that the government would be responsible for damages caused by a failure to do so.[27] For example, the court held that compensation must be paid to the extent that road construction diminished the value of an owner's premises by lowering a street and negligently leaving abutting land elevated, insecure, and unsupported.[28]

In typical situations involving street improvements, the North Carolina courts have been disinclined to require compensation for grade changes, even when the abutter must incur substantial construction costs to reestablish access. For example, in *Smith v. State Highway Commission*,[29] a town changed a street's elevation in connection with sewer installation, which increased the grade of the subject street by between six and thirteen feet. To connect the affected property owners' land to the road, "a ramp would have to be built, which would extend about 35 feet into petitioners' property at the northwest corner where the height of the fill is 6.1 feet, and it would have to extend about 46 feet onto petitioners' property at the northeast corner where the height of the fill is 12.8 feet."[30] The North Carolina Supreme Court said that even under these circumstances, "[a]ny diminution of access by an abutting landowner is *damnum absque injuria* [(loss without injury)]."[31] The court also said that "[t]he public has a paramount right to improve the highway for highway purposes."[32]

While the cases often seem to insulate municipalities from claims to compensation for any changes in grade, no reported case has involved facts in which a change was allowed without compensation when it became impossible or extremely impractical for the abutter to continue to access the road. In *Smith*, discussed above, the most recent North Carolina Supreme Court case directly addressing the issue, the court spoke of "incidental interference" and "conformity with plans to promote public convenience"[33] as circumstances that do not implicate a compensation requirement. It is difficult to imagine a realistic situation today in which a change in grade would make property entirely inaccessible and the courts would deem the outcome to be merely incidental.

---

26. *E.g., Dorsey*, 148 N.C. 423, 62 S.E. 547; Meares v. Comm'rs of Wilmington, 31 N.C. 73 (1848).

27. *Meares*, 31 N.C. at 81.

28. Harper v. Town of Lenoir, 152 N.C. 723, 725–30, 68 S.E. 228, 229–31 (1910).

29. 257 N.C. 410, 126 S.E.2d 87.

30. *Id.* at 412, 126 S.E.2d at 89.

31. *Id.* at 414, 126 S.E.2d at 90.

32. *Id.* at 415, 126 S.E.2d at 91.

33. *Id.* at 413–16, 126 S.E.2d at 89–92.

5.3 Control and Maintenance

A municipality's power over its streets is a matter of legislatively delegated statutory authority.[34] Included within the provisions of G.S. 160A-296, which addresses municipal control of streets, are two specific duties: "to keep the public streets, sidewalks, alleys, and bridges open for travel and free from unnecessary obstructions" and "to keep the public streets, sidewalks, alleys, and bridges in proper repair."[35] These duties are grounded in common law. As the North Carolina Court of Appeals summarized, "municipalities have the positive duty to maintain their streets and sidewalks in a safe condition and keep them free of unnecessary obstructions and are civilly liable for negligently failing to discharge that duty."[36]

Basic decisions about what roads a municipality should open are within the municipality's discretion. As the North Carolina Supreme Court said: "A city or town may in its discretion accept or reject an offer of dedication; it has the right to determine where its streets shall be located. It may accept a part of a street and determine the width of the street, and the width need not conform to the offer of dedication."[37] For such discretionary matters, a municipality has sovereign immunity from liability for damages, though a municipality waives this immunity to the extent of its liability insurance.[38] A municipality is not immunized from all liability for negligence. As the North Carolina Court of Appeals explained, "municipalities may exercise their discretion, while remaining subject to protection from liability by the doctrine of governmental immunity, in deciding which roads to keep open for vehicular traffic and which roads should not continue to be open for such travel. However, in the event that the municipality decides to allow travel on a particular street or road, governmental immunity is not available as a defense to any claim arising from personal injuries or property damage sustained as a result of a defective condition in the maintenance of that street or road."[39]

Those who use streets, and the municipalities that maintain them, do not always agree on the difference between discretionary matters for which sovereign immunity exists and negligence for which a municipality is responsible. For example, decisions about street lighting are, in general, discretionary matters. A municipality may face liability, however, if it installs lighting in a way that creates a dangerous condition. As the North Carolina Supreme Court explained: "It is the existence

---

34. Town of Emerald Isle v. State, 320 N.C. 640, 656, 360 S.E.2d 756, 766 (1987).

35. G.S. 160A-296(a)(1)–(2).

36. McDonald v. Vill. of Pinehurst, 91 N.C. App. 633, 635, 372 S.E.2d 733, 734 (1988).

37. Wofford v. N.C. State Highway Comm'n, 263 N.C. 677, 684, 140 S.E.2d 376, 381 (1965) (citations omitted).

38. Lunsford v. Renn, 207 N.C. App. 298, 308, 700 S.E.2d 94, 100 (2010).

39. Kirkpatrick v. Town of Nags Head, 213 N.C. App. 132, 142, 713 S.E.2d 151, 158 (2011).

of the danger, not its origin, with which the unwarned traveller is concerned, and which engages the attention of the safety laws. A municipality cannot, with impunity, create in its streets a condition palpably dangerous, neglect to provide the most ordinary means of protection against it, and avoid liability for proximate injury on the plea of governmental immunity."[40]

The North Carolina Supreme Court instructed that municipalities must "use ordinary care not only in protecting dangerous places in the street itself, but also to cover dangerous places near the street or highway" with a guard rail or some other barrier or device to address an unreasonably dangerous condition.[41] The court also said that a municipality is required to "keep its streets free of unnecessary obstructions—[in this case] untrimmed shrubs and bushes that obstructed the view of motorists using the streets involved—and so far as we can determine municipalities in this State have never been immune from civil liability for such negligence."[42] A municipality may trim or remove trees on a street if doing so is necessary for construction or maintenance of the street.[43] As the North Carolina Supreme Court said, "The city for the purpose of its government and management can, in its discretion, cut down or trim up the trees bordering the streets, and cannot be restrained unless in cases of willfulness or oppression."[44] A municipality may be responsible for failing to attend to overhanging limbs and foliage that obscure a stop sign if it has been negligent in failing to inspect and maintain the sign.[45] As the court said, "An obstruction can be anything, including vegetation, which renders the public passageway less convenient or safe for use."[46] "Obstructions" on which liability might be based in this sense do not include matters that a municipality does not control, such as traffic.[47]

Minor defects—such as unevenness of one inch in a sidewalk—are deemed too trivial as a matter of law, even if standards might call for greater uniformity and even if some people have been tripped up by them.[48] As the North Carolina Court of Appeals explained, a municipality is "under a duty to use due care to keep its streets and sidewalks in a reasonably safe condition for the ordinary use thereof.' A city will not be liable for injuries caused by '[t]rivial defects, which are

---

40. Hunt v. City of High Point, 226 N.C. 74, 77, 36 S.E.2d 694, 696 (1946).
41. Willis v. City of New Bern, 191 N.C. 507, 511–12, 132 S.E. 286, 288 (1926).
42. McDonald v. Vill. of Pinehurst, 91 N.C. App. 633, 635, 372 S.E.2d 733, 734 (1988).
43. Brown v. Elec. Light Co., 138 N.C. 533, 542, 51 S.E. 62, 65 (1905).
44. Moore v. Carolina Power & Light Co., 163 N.C. 300, 302, 79 S.E. 596, 597 (1913).
45. Stancill v. City of Washington, 29 N.C. App. 707, 709–10, 225 S.E.2d 834, 836 (1976).
46. Cooper v. Town of Southern Pines, 58 N.C. App. 170, 174, 293 S.E.2d 235, 237 (1982).
47. Parker v. Town of Erwin, 243 N.C. App. 84, 107, 776 S.E.2d 710, 727 (2015).
48. Strickland v. City of Raleigh, 204 N.C. App. 176, 179–82, 693 S.E.2d 214, 216–18 (2010).

not inherently dangerous.' Municipalities do not insure that the condition of its streets and sidewalks are at all times absolutely safe."[49]

Land subject to public street rights is usually wider than the paved portion of the street. Municipalities have discretion to use the additional space as a shoulder or for a sidewalk, signs, or drainage. Or it may merely be kept clear from construction. Despite a municipality's discretion to use the entire width of a right of way for travel purposes if it chooses to do so, the property owners along the road may have trees, shrubs, and other landscaping, as well as things such as mailboxes, outside the paved area but within the right of way. An owner's right to make improvements to this area, such as to install driveways or culverts, is subject to the government's regulatory powers, and permits usually must be obtained based on satisfaction of conditions. Local regulations also may require landowners to keep the area within a right of way in a safe condition, including by trimming trees and removing obstructions to vision and public travel. An abutter is not entitled to compensation if the improvements must be removed when a street is widened.[50]

A municipality may be responsible for the upkeep of a sidewalk along a state-maintained road within the municipality, unless the state agrees to take over that maintenance. The North Carolina Court of Appeals noted that "the applicable statutes and regulations governing maintenance of roadways define all of the different *components* of the roadway separately—such as pavements, storm drainage or storm sewers, open drainage, shoulders, and sidewalks."[51] An abutter who creates or maintains an unreasonably dangerous condition in a sidewalk may be liable for injuries the abutter causes.[52] Similarly, a municipality does not automatically assume responsibility for improvements that are connected to its systems. For instance, a municipality is not responsible for private sewer lines just because it approves the private lines or ties them into the municipality's system. As the North Carolina Court of Appeals explained, "The general rule in this State is that 'there is no municipal responsibility for maintenance and upkeep of drains and culverts constructed by third persons for their own convenience and the better enjoyment of their property unless such facilities be accepted or controlled in some legal manner by the municipality.'"[53]

---

49. Desmond v. City of Charlotte, 142 N.C. App. 590, 592, 544 S.E.2d 269, 271 (2001) (citations omitted) (quoting Mosseller v. Asheville, 267 N.C. 104, 107, 109, 147 S.E.2d 558, 561–62 (1966)).

50. City of Salisbury v. Barnhardt, 249 N.C. 549, 555–56, 107 S.E.2d 297, 301–02 (1959).

51. Steele v. City of Durham, 245 N.C. App. 318, 323, 782 S.E.2d 331, 334–35 (2016) (emphasis in original).

52. Dunning v. Forsyth Warehouse Co., 272 N.C. 723, 725, 158 S.E.2d 893, 895 (1968).

53. First Gaston Bank of N.C. v. City of Hickory, 203 N.C. App. 195, 204, 691 S.E.2d 715, 722 (2010) (quoting Johnson v. City of Winston-Salem, 239 N.C. 697, 707, 81 S.E.2d 153, 160 (1954)).

6

Closing Streets

Municipalities are statutorily empowered "to close any street or alley either permanently or temporarily" within their jurisdictions.[1] The typical circumstance in which a municipality closes a street is when development occurs in such a way that the public no longer needs to use it because a different street configuration has replaced it. This may result, for example, from a multi-use development project or a major subdivision.

Permanently closing a street has two principal effects: it terminates the public's right to use the route, and abutters get title to the land formerly subject to that right. Municipalities have the power to take lesser measures to change street use. By statute, municipalities "may by ordinance prohibit, regulate, divert, control, and limit pedestrian or vehicular traffic upon the public streets, sidewalks, alleys, and bridges."[2] Consequently, they may reconfigure the paved portion of a right of way, temporarily close it to public travel, or barricade it as a traffic-control measure. The courts presume that such measures are reasonable and will not interfere with a municipality's exercise of discretion in the absence of clear evidence of bad faith.[3]

A state statute requires that a permitting process be followed for the intermittent closing of a street upon request by the governing board of a drainage, watershed improvement, or soil and water conservation district. This process involves public notice by publication and notice to utilities and public carriers.[4]

The statute setting out the requirements for permanently closing a street makes no distinction based on whether a municipality owns the fee or holds an easement in the land over which the street has run. The vast majority of streets are within easements, which were acquired expressly or by acceptance of an implied offer of dedication. The statute is not entirely clear about whether the same procedures apply when the municipality owns the fee. In the absence of any qualification that they do not apply, the more careful approach is to follow them. This approach takes into account that the statute requires a municipality's governing body to consider whether or not "the closing would be detrimental to the public interest" and prohibits closure when the street is necessary for a "reasonable means of ingress and

---

1. Chapter 160A, Section 296(4) of the North Carolina General Statutes (hereinafter G.S.).
2. G.S. 160A-300.
3. Gene's, Inc. v. City of Charlotte, 259 N.C. 118, 121, 129 S.E.2d 889, 892 (1963).
4. G.S. 160A-299.1.

egress" to an abutter's property, which are necessary considerations regardless of the form of the municipality's interest in the right of way.[5]

The procedure for a street closing is statutory. With the comprehensive revision of North Carolina's municipal statutes in 1971,[6] the General Assembly instituted a simple procedure for a municipality to close a street that has become unnecessary for public access. This procedure, described in section 6.3, *infra*, ensures that abutters will receive prior notice and an opportunity to object. The statute also prescribes how title passes after a street has been permanently closed. This result is described in section 6.4, *infra*.

6.1 What Streets a Municipality May Close Permanently

A municipality may vacate any street located either within its boundaries or within its extraterritorial land-use jurisdiction. If the street is under the control of the state Department of Transportation, it cannot be closed without the department's consent.[7] A board of county commissioners may request that the state abandon "any road in the secondary system when the best interest of the people of the county will be served thereby."[8] The department will close the road upon such a request "if in its opinion the public interest demands it."[9] A county also is statutorily authorized to close permanently any public road or easement within its jurisdiction, and not within a municipality or under the department's control, using a notice and public hearing process similar to the statutory procedure for municipalities and subject to the same conditions regarding public interest and necessity.[10] With this procedure, counties can clear title to public streets shown on plats and vest the underlying land in abutters, as described in section 6.4, *infra*.

In general, just as decisions about opening and improving streets are within a municipal council's discretion,[11] the decision about whether to close a street is not subject to legal challenge except "in instances of fraud or oppression constituting a manifest abuse of discretion."[12] However, state law prohibits closing a street on

---

5. G.S. 160A-299(a).

6. 1971 N.C. Sess. Laws ch. 698, § 1.

7. G.S. 160A-299(e).

8. G.S. 136-63(a).

9. *Id.*

10. G.S. 153A-241.

11. Wood v. Duke Land & Improvement Co., 165 N.C. 367, 370, 81 S.E. 422, 423 (1914).

12. Sanders v. Atl. Coast Line R.R. Co., 216 N.C. 312, 315, 4 S.E.2d 902, 904 (1939).

which a landowner depends for reasonable access to the public road system, an action that, as described in section 5.1, *supra*, could entitle the landowner to compensation for diminished property value. When there is no such need for a street, and the council determines that the street closing is in the public interest, the council may close it by complying with the notice, hearing, and recording procedure set forth in G.S. 160A-299 and described in section 6.3, *infra*.

G.S. 160A-299 does not expressly address whether it applies if a municipality is closing only portions of a street or alley. However, the North Carolina Court of Appeals expressly held that the statute contemplates partial closings.[13] The North Carolina Supreme Court said the same about an earlier version of the statute.[14] There is no reason to believe that the General Assembly would insist that the full length and width of a street be maintained when the conditions for a closing set out in G.S. 160A-299 are met.

G.S. 160A-299(d) states that the closing procedure requirements apply to "any street or alley within a city or its extraterritorial jurisdiction that has been irrevocably dedicated to the public, without regard to whether it has actually been opened," as well as "to unopened streets or public alleys that are shown on plats but that have not been accepted or maintained by the city, provided that this section shall not abrogate the rights of a dedicator, or those claiming under a dedicator, pursuant to G.S. 136-96." The meaning of this language—applying a "closing" process to something that was never opened—is not entirely clear. The following is what seems to be the most logical interpretation in view of the common law governing public rights of way.

The first sentence of G.S. 160A-299(d) applies the closing procedure requirements to any street "irrevocably dedicated to the public" but not opened. This seems to apply when landowners have relied on use of a subdivision road but the municipality has not taken control over it. The North Carolina Supreme Court has held that if a right of way was deemed offered for dedication, it becomes available for a municipality to add it to its network of public streets, "to be opened and subjected to regulation as the growth of the city demands."[15] Subsection (d) enables a municipality to terminate any such lingering availability for acceptance.

The first sentence of subsection (d) also seems to apply to portions of rights of way that are deemed accepted but that have not been opened as streets. When an offer of dedication has been accepted, either expressly or with the opening of a

---

13. Williamson v. Town of Surf City, 143 N.C. App. 539, 544 n.1, 545 S.E.2d 798, 801 n.1 (2001).

14. Wofford v. N.C. State Highway Comm'n, 263 N.C. 677, 684, 140 S.E.2d 376, 382 (1965).

15. Bailliere v. Atl. Shingle Cooperage & Veneer Co., 150 N.C. 627, 638, 64 S.E. 754, 759 (1909).

street, public rights attach to the full width of the land that was offered, including any portion that has not actually been put to use.[16] The statute enables a municipality to extinguish rights in those unused portions.

The second sentence of G.S. 160A-299(d) applies the closing procedure "to unopened streets or public alleys that are shown on plats but that have not been accepted or maintained by the city, provided that this section shall not abrogate the rights of a dedicator, or those claiming under a dedicator, pursuant to G.S. 136-96." As described in section 2.4, *supra*, G.S. 136-96 enables a developer to withdraw an offer of dedication if a street has not been opened within fifteen years and the developer thereafter files a declaration of withdrawal. The second sentence of subsection (d) appears to give municipalities a procedure to terminate the possibility of acceptance before the fifteen years has run, as well as after fifteen years if the dedicator does not act after fifteen years or cannot be found. This may be appropriate, for example, if subdivision landowners want to clear title to land shown as a street on the plat but never used as such.

Situations arise in which a landowner discovers evidence of a possible claim to a public street that is not shown on any plat and the municipality involved has no record of having accepted or maintained any such street. As described in sections 2.2 and 3.3, *supra*, public use alone does not automatically make an intended right of way a public street. A municipality may reasonably conclude that G.S. 160A-299 does not apply in such situations. This interpretation avoids the implications of the conclusive abutter vesting rules that follow a closing under G.S. 160A-299, as described in section 6.4 *infra*, which may not be consistent with record title to the abutters' land. A landowner who wants to settle a claim of possible public rights under such circumstances may instead need to bring a quiet title action to obtain a decree that can be recorded in the register of deeds office.

6.2 Conditions for Closing Streets

Before a municipality can legally close a street permanently, its council must be satisfied of two conditions: that the closing is "not contrary to the public interest" and that no one who owns property in the vicinity of the street will be deprived of "reasonable means of ingress and egress" to that property after the street is closed.[17]

---

16. Home Real Estate Loan & Ins. Co. v. Town of Carolina Beach, 216 N.C. 778, 787, 7 S.E.2d 13, 20 (1940); March v. Town of Kill Devil Hills, 125 N.C. App. 151, 153, 479 S.E.2d 252, 253 (1997).

17. G.S. 160A-299(a).

The public interest consideration that a municipal council must consider incorporates the essence of common law that the purpose of municipal streets is to serve the public. However, the statutory formulation—*"not contrary* to the public interest"—recognizes that closing streets affects both public and private interests. A municipality's release of a street is often accompanied by questions as to the particular usefulness of the land to its abutting owners. As long as a public interest is served, the fact of parallel private benefit should not bar a street closure. Among the other public considerations that may be relevant are how a closure could affect traffic flow on other streets and whether the street might be needed in the future to accommodate growth or other change.

Allowing the closure of a public right of way only if it is not needed for reasonable abutter road access is consistent with the common law principle that a road cannot be withdrawn from an offer of dedication without compensation to an abutter who needs it.[18] To comply with state law, a municipal council should examine a subject street's location in relation to properties in the vicinity to ensure that a closing would not cut landowners off from access to public roads. This consideration likely will have been addressed in a report from the municipality's planning department. G.S. 160A-299 allows closure if abutters will be left with another "reasonable means of ingress and egress." Similar to considering the requirement of reasonable alternative access, which allows an offer of dedication to be withdrawn, as discussed in section 2.4, *supra*, reasonable access in this context would likely be deemed available if there is a reasonably direct and open alternative connection to the public road network. However, landowners should not have to acquire an additional right of way from a neighbor or install an alternative driveway at significant cost.

A court will reverse a municipal council's determination about public interest and reasonable alternative access for individuals owning property near a subject street only if, based on the record that was presented to the council, the council is found to have acted arbitrarily or capriciously.[19] To demonstrate that it has been reasonable in its determinations, the council should enable interested parties to offer evidence on the statutory considerations at the public hearing on the matter and state on the record the facts on which it determined that the conditions for a closing were met.

---

18. Steadman v. Town of Pinetops, 251 N.C. 509, 515–16, 112 S.E.2d 102, 107 (1960).
19. Houston v. Town of Chapel Hill, 177 N.C. App. 739, 741, 630 S.E.2d 249, 252 (2006).

6.3 Street-Closing Procedure

A North Carolina municipality must comply with the General Statutes procedure to close a street permanently. While some municipalities have their own processes for landowners to follow when filing a petition to initiate a public street closing, all municipalities are responsible for complying with the notice, hearing, filing, and other requirements set out in G.S. 160A-299(a). The steps in this procedure are straightforward.

A municipality formally begins a street closing procedure when its council adopts a resolution declaring its intent to close the street and calling a public hearing on the matter. The resolution should precisely define the street or street portion to be closed. This description will be important for determining boundaries if the closing occurs, and it is important for identifying the landowners who are entitled to notice of the closure proposal.

A municipality may not close a street without complying with the notice requirements found in G.S. 160A-299(a).[20] The statute requires the municipality to send a copy of the resolution to close the street "by registered or certified mail to all owners of property adjoining the street or alley as shown on the county tax records" and also mandates that "a notice of the closing and public hearing shall be prominently posted in at least two places along the street or alley."[21] This is intended to notify "a landowner whose property is affected by the change, and who will suffer some peculiar and special injury by reason of it[,]" about the proposed street closing.[22] The statute allows a municipality to rely on tax records for purposes of determining parties to whom the resolution must be sent, even though the tax records may not reflect current title based on register of deeds filings. Due process concerns about any gaps in the provision of notice by mail are likely alleviated by the requirements that the closure resolution be published according to specific frequency and duration terms and that notice of the closing and public hearing on the matter be posted along the subject street. It follows that a municipality is not required to supplement a mailing of notices if it learns of a property transfer after the notices were sent based on the tax record information. Notice also must be given to the state Department of Transportation if the street is under the department's authority and control.[23] G.S. 160A-299(a) does not state how far in advance of the hearing the notices must be mailed, but, logically, they should be sent at the outset of the publication process described in the next paragraph.

---

20. Town of Blowing Rock v. Gregorie, 243 N.C. 364, 372, 90 S.E.2d 898, 904 (1956).
21. G.S. 160A-299(a).
22. Shaw v. Liggett & Myers Tobacco Co., 226 N.C. 477, 477–78, 38 S.E.2d 313, 313 (1946).
23. G.S. 160A-299(a).

A street closure resolution must be published "once a week for four successive weeks" before the hearing on the street closing before the municipal council. G.S. 1-597 has rules for identifying a suitable newspaper for providing this notice. As the North Carolina Court of Appeals explained, "A newspaper of general circulation is a publication to which the general public would resort in order to be informed of the news and intelligence of the day, editorial opinions, and advertisements, and thereby to render it probable that the 'notice' would be brought to the attention of the general public."[24]

Although the statutory language about the timing of required publications is not entirely clear, the cautious approach is to publish the notice of hearing on the same day of the week in four successive calendar weeks, with the hearing scheduled for not earlier than the calendar week following the calendar week of the fourth publication.[25] Publication notice should be sufficient as long as publication is made in four successive calendar weeks and the hearing occurs after the fourth publication. The statute does not state that, after publication is complete, a certain number of days must elapse before the hearing can be held, as is the case with other statutes that clearly require a span of time after the last hearing and before the event it describes.[26] Nor does the statute say *not less than* once a week for four successive weeks," which is language that the North Carolina Supreme Court once interpreted as referring to a "space of time" of substantially twenty-eight days, not merely once a week in four successive weeks.[27] The United States Supreme Court once said that "once a week for four successive weeks" means four notices in successive weeks and not necessarily within a period of at least twenty-eight days.[28] As another state supreme court put it when considering a "successive weeks" measure, when a legislature desires an "interval to elapse between publication and the event publicized, it knows how to express itself."[29] Still, despite this possible authority for having the hearing any time after the final publication, the more cautious approach is to schedule the hearing for no sooner than the calendar week following the calendar week of the fourth publication.

---

24. Great S. Media, Inc. v. McDowell Cty., 50 N.C. App. 705, 719, 275 S.E.2d 226, 234 (1981).

25. *See* Sullivan v. Faria, 308 A.2d 473, 476 (R.I. 1973) (interpreting similar language).

26. *E.g.,* G.S. 45-21.17(2)(b) (for foreclosure sale notice, "[t]he date of the last publication shall be not more than 10 days preceding the date of the sale"); 143-318.12(b)(2) (public notice of a special meeting must be complete at least forty-eight hours before the meeting).

27. S.D. Scott & Co. v. Jones, 230 N.C. 74, 78, 52 S.E.2d 219, 221–22 (1949).

28. Early v. Doe, 57 U.S. 610, 616–17 (1853).

29. *Sullivan*, 308 A.2d at 476.

At the hearing, the relevant subjects are the two statutory conditions[30] described in section 6.2, *supra*, that, if not met, would prevent the closure of a street. The council in a municipality should give both abutters and the public an opportunity to offer information to the council about these conditions. However, the council should consider the conditions and decide on the record whether they exist regardless of whether anyone else raises them during the public hearing. If the council votes to close the street, the order should make a specific finding about each of the two conditions, as well as precisely describe the portion of the road to be closed consistent with the resolution. If the council decides at the hearing that a different portion of the street should be closed than had been advertised, a new notice and hearing process should be recommenced.

G.S. 160A-299(b) permits appeal of a council's closing order to the superior court by "[a]ny person aggrieved" by the closing. Presumably, this language codifies the case law that limits challenges of street closings to persons "whose property is affected by the change" in a "peculiar and special" way, which likely is limited to any owner of property whose direct access is affected.[31] The North Carolina Court of Appeals held that someone who is three blocks away from, or is merely a public user of, the subject street is not a "person aggrieved" entitled to appeal under the statute.[32] Any appeal must be taken within thirty days after the street closing order is adopted.[33] The court of appeals held that the thirty-day appeal requirement applied even to an abutter who claimed not to have received the statutorily required notice.[34] The statute prohibits collateral attack of the closing order in other litigation. It states, "No cause of action or defense founded on the invalidity of the proceedings taken in closing any street or alley may be asserted, nor shall the validity of the order be open to question in any court upon any ground whatever," except in an appeal from the order.[35]

On appeal, the judge, sitting without a jury, will review the council's compliance with the notice and other procedural requirements in the statute.[36] The statute limits the consideration of additional evidence to review of the council's compli-

---

30. (1) The street closure is "not contrary to the public interest" and (2) abutters will not be deprived of "reasonable means of ingress and egress" to their property should the street be closed.

31. Shaw v. Liggett & Myers Tobacco Co., 226 N.C. 477, 477–78, 38 S.E.2d 313, 313 (1946).

32. Cox v. Town of Oriental, 234 N.C. App. 675, 679, 759 S.E.2d 388, 391 (2014).

33. G.S. 160A-299(b).

34. Groves v. Cmty Hous. Corp. of Haywood Cty., 144 N.C. App. 79, 88, 548 S.E.2d 535, 541 (2001).

35. G.S. 160A-299(b).

36. *Id.*

ance with the procedural requirements.[37] The North Carolina Court of Appeals explained that this means that parties may not "present new evidence concerning whether closing the street or alley is contrary to the public interest, whether an aggrieved individual would be deprived of reasonable means of ingress and egress to his property, or whether the council's decision was in accordance with any other applicable requirements of local law or ordinance."[38] If the court finds that the council complied with the procedural requirements, it will overrule the council's determination on public interest and reasonable access only if, based on the record that was presented to the council, it finds that the council acted arbitrarily or capriciously.[39]

As a final step in the street closing procedure, a certified copy of the closing order must be filed in the register of deeds' office in every county in which the closed street is situated.[40] This order will be the basis for concluding that the street is no longer subject to public rights, except as expressly reserved in the order, and for proof that the former street land has vested in abutters, as described in the next section.

6.4 Vesting of Title after Closing

Once a municipality permanently closes a street, G.S. 160A-299(c) provides that "all right, title, and interest in the right-of-way shall be conclusively presumed to be vested" in the abutting landowners, each taking to the center of the street. There are two exceptions.

One exception is that the statute authorizes abutting landowners to agree among themselves on what their mutual property boundaries will be after closure. This alternative requires the "assent of all property owners taking title to a closed street or alley," which is accomplished by means of a plat that all owners must sign, to be recorded with the register of deeds.[41] The owners could achieve the same result with a boundary agreement among themselves after the process, but the statute authorizes the making of such alternative arrangements during the process, dispensing with possible subdivision or other regulatory approval requirements.

---

37. *Id.*
38. Houston v. Town of Chapel Hill, 177 N.C. App. 739, 743, 630 S.E.2d 249, 253 (2006).
39. *Id.* at 741, 630 S.E.2d at 252.
40. G.S. 160A-299(a).
41. G.S. 160A-299(c).

As for the second exception to the rule set out in G.S. 160A-299(c), the statute provides that "[a] city may reserve a right, title, and interest in any improvements or easements within a street closed pursuant to this section."[42] To make this reservation, a municipality should identify the reservation in the order of closure that is recorded with the register of deeds.

The statute says that title is "conclusively presumed to be vested" in abutters to the center of the street. A presumption of equal division reflects the common law rule that, in general, when a street is used as a boundary line in a deed description, the conveyance is construed to be to the center of the street.[43] This presumption follows from the likelihood that a right of way would be put where it can serve lots on both sides, and a developer would not want to reserve separate ownership rights to a narrow strip.[44] However, at common law, and in other states, courts and legislatures usually have made the presumption of a centerline allocation a rebuttable one.[45] For example, the North Carolina statutory rule for abandoned railroad easements extends side property lines to the centerline but makes this presumption "rebuttable by showing that a party has a good and valid title to the land."[46] The presumption might be rebutted, for example, if a sub-divider set aside land for a street along the side of the subdivision rather than through its interior. Having a rebuttable presumption prevents an owner who had sole vested title in a manner such as this from having property reassigned differently after a street closing. As the North Carolina Supreme Court once said, quoting the United States Supreme Court, "We know of no case in which a legislative Act to transfer the property from A to B without his consent has ever been a constitutional exercise of the legislative power in any State in the Union."[47] The drafters of G.S. 160A-299 apparently favored a simple process that would not embroil a municipal council in factual determinations about title before a street was opened over an approach that focused on the concern that an owner with record title could challenge a different vesting as an unconstitutional taking of property.[48] The drafters may logically have

---

42. G.S. 160A-299(f).

43. Goss v. Stidhams, 68 N.C. App. 773, 776, 315 S.E.2d 777, 778 (1984).

44. *See* Woodman v. Spencer, 54 N.H. 507, 511 (1874) (explaining the presumption).

45. *See, e.g.,* Duchesnaye v. Silva, 394 A.2d 59, 61 (N.H. 1978) ("conveyance of property bounded by a street or highway normally conveys title to the center of the boundary street, unless clearly contrary language appears in the deed"); Cal. Civ. Code § 831 (2018) ("An owner of land bounded by a road or street is presumed to own to the center of the way, but the contrary may be shown.").

46. G.S. 1-44.2.

47. Trs. of the Univ. of N.C. v. N.C. R.R. Co., 76 N.C. 103, 107 (1877) (quoting Wilkinson v. Leland, 27 U.S. 627, 657–58 (1829)).

48. *See* McDonald's Corp v. Dwyer, 338 N.C. 445, 449, 450 S.E.2d 888, 891 (1994) (holding that a statute requiring a landowner to challenge a presumption that title

assumed that the conclusive presumption would lead to the right result in the vast majority of cases and that, even when it did not, the affected landowners likely would not have expected a different result and the economic effect of the result would not be substantial.

The statute on vesting of title after a street closing does not specifically address how it applies if the subject street has been narrowed by closing a part of it along one of its sides rather than by closing the street for its full width. The most logical interpretation is that title vests in an abutter in any area up to the centerline at the time of the closing. This could result in realignment of future vesting rights because a new centerline will be established, but it is consistent with the presumption of ownership to the centerline for the particular closing. Another configuration not specifically addressed in the statute is how to draw the boundaries for a closed cul-de-sac, with respect to which abutters have frontages that converge if their sidelines are extended into the closed street. A cul-de-sac is unlikely to be closed because the abutting properties typically use it as their only access to the road system. If such a rarity arose, the most rational interpretation is that title vests in abutters in a manner similar to the traditional approach for riparian rights in circular ponds or lakes, which is to extend sidelines to the cul-de-sac's center point, creating a shape similar to pie slices, with each abutter getting a slice.[49]

Title in land after a street closure vests by operation of law when a council's closure order is recorded with the register of deeds.[50] Accordingly, there is no requirement or need to record deeds of conveyance. If a municipality is one of the fee-owning abutters, it acquires title the same way as a private party and may devote the land to other public uses.[51]

vests in abutters to the centerline of an abandoned railroad easement was in effect an unconstitutional conclusive presumption).

49. *See, e.g.,* Hanson v. Rice, 92 N.W. 982, 983 (Minn. 1903) (stating the rule).

50. General Greene Inv. Co. v. Greene, 48 N.C. App. 29, 35, 268 S.E.2d 810, 814 (1980).

51. Williamson v. Town of Surf City, 143 N.C. App. 539, 543–44, 545 S.E.2d 798, 800–01 (2001).

7

Utilities and Railroad Crossings

A typical modern street includes not only pavement for vehicles and a sidewalk for pedestrians but also poles, lines, and pipes for public utilities such as water, sewer, gas, telephone, and data. A municipality's authority to accept offers of dedication includes the ability to accept them for utility lines.[1] Commonly, a municipal or other public utility relies on permission from a municipality or other government unit to use its public street easement by license. Issues sometimes arise about the municipality's right to authorize utilities within a street or other easement. The municipality's control and maintenance of its streets may also intersect with a railroad line, a relationship that is subject to both statutory and common law rules for allocating responsibility.

7.1 Utilities within Scope of Easement

There is no serious question about the use of municipal property for utilities if the municipality owns the land in fee. Under these circumstances, the municipality has the entire bundle of property interests in the subject street, and state statutes expressly authorize municipalities to license utility facilities in street rights of way.[2] Furthermore, the North Carolina General Statutes authorize electric, telephone, and telegraph utilities to place their lines in street rights of way if the lines do not constitute an obstruction.[3] Thus, municipalities may not deny a license to any public utility looking to install lines unless an obstruction will result.

When the municipality has an easement for a street rather than owning the underlying fee, questions may arise about the municipality's right to install utility lines, or to enter into agreements with utility providers to install their lines, within the street easement. The owner of the fee, or the abutters who have a reversionary interest in ownership if the street is closed, may challenge an installation as an additional burden for which compensation must be paid. A municipality can

---

1. Chapter 160A, Section 374 of the North Carolina General Statutes (hereinafter G.S.).
2. G.S. 160A-296.
3. G.S. 62-180.

foreclose such claims by explicitly including the right to install utilities within the terms of an easement conveyance or offer of dedication. State statutes permit a subdivision control ordinance to provide for the dedication of "rights-of-way or easements for street and utility purposes,"[4] and an ordinance could provide that a single easement would permit both sorts of public use. Older streets, however, may not have the benefit of such clear authorization. They may be maintained pursuant to easement conveyances that were more narrowly expressed, and, in such circumstances, the fee owner or abutter may contend that other uses would be an additional burden for which compensation is required, even though the economic impact of such utilities may be negligible or actually enhance property values.

When the easement language is not narrowly confined to street use, a court is likely to deem utilities included within the permitted scope of the easement rights. In the early 1897 case of *Smith v. City of Goldsboro*,[5] a developer had offered to dedicate "streets" to the public by platting a subdivision with streets and selling lots as shown on the plat. When the city accepted the streets, and planned to run water pipes and electric lines within the street easements, the dedicator sought compensation for these additional uses, contending that the allowed use was only as "county roads" and not as an "urban way." The North Carolina Supreme Court held that the municipality acquired the "streets" not only for travel but also to furnish water and lights—that is, for all purposes to which cities normally put them.[6]

More recent cases take a similarly broad view of what rights are included in offers of dedication. In *Watkins v. Lambe-Young, Inc.*,[7] the North Carolina Court of Appeals held that a street easement dedicated "for public use" permitted the laying of a water line in the street without creating an additional compensable burden. The court noted, "Where the owner delivers land to a public use in such manner that his acts would fairly and reasonably lead an ordinarily prudent man to infer that he intended to dedicate the land to that use, acceptance of the land by some public body entitled to do so causes the dedication to become irrevocable."[8] Consequently, when the purpose for which an easement was acquired was stated broadly, no compensation is required when the contemplated public use is among those for which the government is statutorily authorized. Both municipalities and the state Department of Transportation are expressly authorized by statute to enter into agreements for utilities to install lines within public streets.[9]

---

4. G.S. 160A-372(a).
5. 121 N.C. 350, 28 S.E. 479 (1897).
6. *Id.* at 352–54, 28 S.E. at 479–80.
7. 37 N.C. App. 30, 245 S.E.2d 202 (1978).
8. *Id.* at 31, 245 S.E.2d at 203–04.
9. G.S. 136-18(2)(c); 160A-296(a).

In some early cases, the North Carolina Supreme Court held that a property owner was entitled to make a case for additional compensation for a utility installation deemed not within the intended scope of an easement. These cases arose around the turn of the twentieth century, as streets and utilities were rapidly expanding along with land development, and landowners arguably had more confined reasonable expectations about what a street might entail than they do now. In the 1893 case of *White v. Northwestern North Carolina Railroad Co.*,[10] for example, an abutter, who was presumed to own the fee of land over which the public had a street easement, alleged entitlement to compensation when a railroad line was installed, which required extensive changes to the street, including excavation and pillar installation. The North Carolina Supreme Court said that the question was "whether or not the use of a steam railroad is a perversion of the street from its original and proper public purposes" and held that the changes in use were too much.[11] It said that "where the public have only an easement in the street, and the fee of the soil of the street is retained in the abutting owner, a steam railroad cannot, under the constitutional guaranty of private property, be lawfully constructed and operated thereon against his will and without compensation."[12] Similarly, in a 1902 case, *Phillips v. Postal Telegraph-Cable Co.*,[13] the state high court held that a landowner was entitled to make a claim to compensation when a telegraph company installed its lines and poles by agreement with a railroad that had a right of way on the owner's farm. The court noted that the railroad's rights were only for tracks and that the lines and poles were alleged to interfere with farming operations.[14] Installation of utility lines and poles that allegedly interfere with property's use as a farming operation, in an era in which such features were not an integral part of the landscape as they are now, may have seemed to have a more distinctive impact than would today's installation of utilities along streets.

In 1941–42, in separate decisions on two appeals within the same case, both with the caption *Hildebrand v. Southern Bell Telephone & Telegraph Co.*,[15] the North Carolina Supreme Court considered a landowner's claim to compensation stemming from the installation within a highway right of way of telephone poles and lines. By condemnation, the state had acquired the right of way on the landowner's property "for all purposes for which the State Highway and Public Works Commission is authorized by law to subject such right of way" and built a

---

10. 113 N.C. 610, 18 S.E. 330 (1893).
11. *Id.* at 613, 18 S.E. at 331.
12. *Id.* at 616, 18 S.E. at 332.
13. 130 N.C. 513, 41 S.E. 1022 (1902).
14. *Id.* at 523–25, 41 S.E. at 1025–26.
15. 219 N.C. 402, 14 S.E.2d 252 (1941); 221 N.C. 10, 18 S.E.2d 827 (1942).

road.[16] The state highway commission granted a telephone company a license to install poles and wires within the right of way, which the landowner claimed was a trespass.[17] At the time *Hildebrand* was considered, the State Highway and Public Works Commission had regulatory authority over the installation of utilities within its rights of way, but no statutory authority to grant licenses to utilities. Consequently, its condemnation for "right of way" purposes did not include consideration of utility lines as part of that right of way. The court held that the owner could make a claim to compensation. The court also noted, however, that the question of compensation was a matter of economic impact, the determination of which depended on whether the lines had an appreciable effect on the land greater than that of the highway. As the court said,

> It may be conceded that the easement acquired by the State for a public highway is, under existing law, so extensive in nature and the control exercised by the Highway Commission is so exclusive in extent that the subservient estate in the land, from a practical standpoint, amounts to little more than the right of reverter in the event the easement is abandoned. Nevertheless, the subservient estate still exists and any encroachment thereon entitles the owner to nominal damages at least. The fact that the injury may be trivial, though material in determining the amount of the owner's damages, does not affect his constitutional rights or the principle of law involved. He is entitled to be protected as to that which is his without regard to its money value.[18]

This explanation shows that while there were still reasons in the 1940s to take a confined view about what utilities could be included in a street right of way, the courts were recognizing that the utilities might not have an impact that warrants compensation. In 1957, the North Carolina Supreme Court followed similar reasoning in *Grimes v. Virginia Electric & Power Co.*[19] Landowners, who had given a power company a fifty-foot-wide easement right to install electric lines and poles, objected when the company entered into an agreement with a municipality for it to attach its wires and equipment, including a cross-arm, to the poles, as well as the right to enter the property for maintenance. The North Carolina Supreme Court said, in general, "Any additional burden beyond the grant entitles the landowner to just compensation," but whether its effect was measurable was for a jury to determine.[20]

---

16. 221 N.C. at 11, 18 S.E.2d at 828.
17. 219 N.C. at 404–05, 14 S.E.2d at 254.
18. *Id.* at 408, 14 S.E.2d at 256–57.
19. 245 N.C. 583, 96 S.E.2d 713 (1957).
20. *Id.* at 585, 96 S.E.2d at 714.

The North Carolina Supreme Court addressed the compensation question again in 1964 in *Van Leuven v. Akers Motor Lines Inc.*,[21] in which lot owners sought to prevent a neighbor with a trucking business from using their lot to connect to a public sewer. The trucking business obtained a permit from the State Highway Commission for use of the highway right of way for the connection. The court said that a sewer line was not part of the state's highway easement rights and that the lot owners would be entitled to compensation for the economic impact of additional burden to their land caused by the line's installation. The court also noted, "It is proper to show the existence of a pre-existing easement when assessing damages for an additional one in order to limit recovery only for the difference in the fair market value of the land involved subject to the pre-existing easement and immediately after subjecting it to the added burden."[22] Just a few years later, in *City of Randleman v. Hinshaw*,[23] the North Carolina Supreme Court held that a landowner could have a theoretical claim to compensation when a municipality expresses an intention to install its sewer and water lines within a state highway right of way. The state high court again noted, "Of course, in determining the compensation to be paid to the landowner, account must be taken of benefits to his property from the construction of the proposed improvement."[24]

The import of these cases is that, in some circumstances, there could be a compensation obligation if, within an easement, a utility installation is made that was not described in terms that can reasonably be interpreted as including such rights, but this obligation exists only to the extent its impact diminishes the value of the subject property. Today, this issue is most likely to arise only when an easement was obtained for very narrowly defined purposes. With respect to new streets, municipal acquisitions are likely to take into account statutory authority to grant licenses to utilities, which includes authorizing the installation of "pipes, poles, wires, fixtures, or appliances of any kind either on, above, or below the surface" of public streets.[25] With respect to already established streets, the issue of required compensation most likely is theoretical. As the courts have regularly pointed out, as long as a municipality may legally authorize the installation and maintenance of utility lines, there is unlikely to be an appreciable diminished value to abutters. This reality is reflected in relatively more recent cases. For example, in *Mason v. Town of Fletcher*,[26] a trial court found that landowners were not entitled to compensation when a town installed a water line within the state highway easement,

---

21. 261 N.C. 539, 135 S.E.2d 640 (1964).
22. *Id.* at 544–45, 135 S.E.2d at 644.
23. 267 N.C. 136, 147 S.E.2d 902 (1966).
24. *Id.* at 144, 147 S.E.2d at 908.
25. G.S. 160A-296(a)(6).
26. 149 N.C. App. 636, 561 S.E.2d 524 (2002).

even though the installation was not within the permissible scope of the easement. The trial court found that the landowners "suffered no damage, but rather the installation of the water line enhanced the value of their property."[27] The North Carolina Court of Appeals held that the installation was not a trespass because the state had statutory authority to enter into an agreement with the town to install the water line and the line was within the permissible public uses for the right of way.[28] The court did not address the issue of compensation.

Although utilities are now commonly maintained within street rights of way, municipalities also maintain utilities within easements that are solely for utility purposes. A municipality may also continue an easement for utility purposes after discontinuing a street. By statute, a municipality may reserve easements for its own utilities, or for those of other utility companies, in rights of way that a dedicator may withdraw after fifteen years without an opening of the subject street pursuant to G.S. 136-96.[29] To do so, the municipality must first give notice to the party with the power of withdrawal at least five days before a public hearing on the matter. The rights are reserved only if the municipality passes a resolution with a "declaration of retention of utility easements" and with a specific description of the retained easements before any plat of withdrawal is filed. The declaration must be filed with the register of deeds.[30]

Claims to compensation for utility easements also have arisen in cases where a municipality requires a utility company to move its lines. For example, in *Southern Bell Telephone & Telegraph Company v. Housing Authority*,[31] a telephone company sought compensation when it was forced to relocate its lines from a street that was being closed for an urban redevelopment project. The court rejected the company's claim, explaining that "the forced relocation of its facilities is no different, in the context of eminent domain, than the forced relocation of the business of a private tenant after condemnation. And '[i]n North Carolina the taking of land does not contemplate compensation for . . . [the] cost [involved] in moving a business and its attendant personal property to another location.'"[32]

Under current law, a landowner has a short time within which to bring a claim for additional compensation based on an alleged public use beyond what is allowed within the scope of an easement. G.S. 40A-51 sets a two-year statute of limitations for bringing an action against a municipality with eminent domain powers when

---

27. *Id.* at 638, 561 S.E.2d at 526.
28. *Id.* at 641, 561 S.E.2d at 527–28.
29. G.S. 160A-299(g).
30. *Id.*
31. 38 N.C. App. 172, 247 S.E.2d 663 (1978).
32. *Id.* at 175, 247 S.E.2d at 666 (omission by court) (quoting City of King's Mountain v. Cline, 19 N.C. App. 9, 12, 198 S.E.2d 64, 66 (1973)).

property is taken without a condemnation proceeding. G.S. 1-52(17) contains a three-year limitations period for seeking compensation "[a]gainst a public utility, electric or telephone membership corporation, or a municipality for damages or for compensation for right-of-way or use of any lands for a utility service line or lines to serve one or more customers or members." The law is not entirely clear about which of these different limitations periods—two or three years—applies to an allegation that a municipality has taken property by installing utilities without acquiring the right to do so. The shorter two-year period in G.S. Chapter 40A, applicable to municipal eminent domain generally, was enacted in 1981 in the same legislative session as, and only a few days after, the three-year period for utility lines in Chapter 52, without mention that the later provision was meant to repeal the earlier.[33] In a case in which a landowner sought compensation when a railroad licensed the installation of fiber optic cable within its track right of way, a North Carolina federal court noted that "§ 40A-51 is a statute of general applicability whereas § 1-52(17) is a statute of specific applicability that applies to claims against a *subset* of entities who might be subject to inverse condemnation claims."[34] The court decided that "claims based on the allegedly unauthorized installation of telecommunications and other utility lines are forever barred unless the aggrieved landowner brings suit within three years after the line has been constructed."[35] Following this reasoning that the more specific statute applies, the longer three-year period would apply to claims against a municipality asserting a taking by installation of utility lines, whereas the two-year period would apply to other claims of inverse condemnation.

7.2 Use of Utility Easement Area for Other Purposes

A carefully drafted easement agreement, or an eminent domain decree acquiring an easement, should specify the scope of the beneficiary's allowable uses and the landowner's retained rights to enjoy the property subject to those uses. For example, a utility easement likely will give the utility the right to build, maintain, and operate lines. It also will allow the utility to cut trees and vegetation within

---

33. 1981 N.C. Sess. Laws ch. 919; 1981 N.C. Sess. Laws ch. 702.

34. Curtis v. Norfolk S. R.R. Co., No. 1:01CV00869, 2002 U.S. Dist. LEXIS 26196, at *9 (M.D.N.C. Aug. 27, 2002). As noted in section 4.3, *supra*, a reverse condemnation claim may lie when the government occupies or uses a person's property, under circumstances warranting compensation, without first following the eminent domain procedure.

35. *Id.* at *10.

the easement area and on property adjacent to it to the extent such growth is a threat to the safe and reliable operation of a utility line. In addition, the easement agreement will authorize the utility to enter the property by foot and with vehicles for purposes of installation, operation, and maintenance. The agreement likely also will prohibit the landowner from installing structures or other improvements within the easement area, including such things as outbuildings, driveways, wells, fences, and swimming pools.

Despite attempts to craft a clear easement agreement, issues sometimes arise (1) when landowners do not study the agreement before they enter into it or (2) related to successors in title who were not made aware of the details of the agreement before acquiring the property. Such misunderstandings come to the surface when landowners build something that violates prohibitions set out in the agreement. A violation may exist for some time before a utility gives notice of an encroachment and demands that it be corrected, perhaps insisting on removal of any infringing improvements. Modern utility easement agreements typically specify that the utility's right to removal is not waived if not enforced over time. Corrections can be costly to landowners.

A court will interpret an imprecise or unclear easement agreement according to the parties' apparent intent.[36] To the extent that the easement agreement or some other source of easement rights does not specify the scope of permitted use, its scope will be interpreted according what is reasonable.[37] Both the circumstances when an easement was created and the circumstances at the time of use are relevant in determining the easement's scope. The beneficiary of an easement may only use it for its intended purpose and may not damage the landowner's retained interest through actions that are unnecessary for the intended purpose. A rule of reasonableness also applies to the landowner's right to continued use of the property subject to the easement.

A landowner retains the right to use the land subject to an easement in ways that do not interfere unreasonably with the easement beneficiary's reasonable use. Sometimes both interests must be weighed. As the North Carolina Court of Appeals said, quoting the *Restatement of Property*, "'The determination as to what constitutes an unreasonable interference on the part of the possessor of the servient tenement with the use of the land by the owner of the easement depends primarily upon a consideration of the relative advantage to him of his desired use and the disadvantage to the owner of the easement.'"[38] In another case, involv-

---

36. Weyerhaeuser Co. v. Carolina Power & Light Co., 257 N.C. 717, 719, 127 S.E.2d 539, 541 (1962).

37. Carolina Power & Light Co. v. Bowman, 229 N.C. 682, 687, 51 S.E.2d 191, 195 (1949).

38. Williams v. Abernethy, 102 N.C. App. 462, 465, 402 S.E.2d 438, 440 (1991) (quoting Restatement of Property § 481 cmt. a, at 3008 (1944)).

ing a wide power line easement, the court of appeals explained that "the servient tenant may make any use of the land so long as the use (1) does not conflict with the power company's rights, *and* (2) is consistent with the purpose for which the easement was granted, *and* (3) does not interfere with the dominant tenant's free exercise of the easement. These requirements are *conjunctive*, and the landowner must meet all three conditions in order to use the land subject to an easement in the manner it chooses."[39]

The holder of easement rights for utilities will not only have the right to install and maintain lines within the easement, but, unless the easement agreement specifies otherwise, other rights naturally associated with installing and maintaining the lines. For example, the North Carolina Court of Appeals held that a municipality that used eminent domain to acquire an easement for a sewer line also acquired "such rights as are incidental to constructing, maintaining and operating a sewer line across the strip of land in question. Necessarily included would be the right to go on the property whenever necessary to inspect, repair or replace the sewer line."[40] The court described the landowner as retaining "the right to traverse [the easement] freely, to park on it, to landscape it, to grade over it and to use it for any lawful purpose at such time and for so long as such uses do not conflict with the rights" of the municipality.[41] The easement beneficiary must conduct its activities with due regard for the landowner's retained rights. The North Carolina Supreme Court has applied a "general rule" that "[i]t is not only the right but the duty of the owner of an easement to keep it in repair; the owner of the servient tenement is under no duty to maintain or repair it, in the absence of an agreement therefor."[42]

A utility easement beneficiary has twenty years to bring an action against a landowner who is interfering with easement use, pursuant to the statute of limitations for the recovery or possession of real property.[43] The North Carolina Supreme Court held that this longer limitation period applies, rather than the shorter six-year limitation for "incorporeal hereditaments"—intangible rights in land—noting that a longer period made sense because "utility facilities crisscross the state above, on, and beneath the ground. Their accompanying easements are not always readily subject to routine inspection by the owning utility."[44]

---

39. Duke Energy Corp. v. Malcolm, 178 N.C. App. 62, 67, 630 S.E.2d 693, 697 (2006) (emphasis in original).

40. City of Statesville v. Bowles, 6 N.C. App. 124, 130, 169 S.E.2d 467, 471 (1969).

41. *Id.*

42. Green v. Duke Power Co., 305 N.C. 603, 611, 290 S.E.2d 593, 598 (1982) (quoting 25 Am. Jur. 2d *Easements & Licenses* § 85 (1966)).

43. G.S. 1-40; Duke Energy Carolinas, LLC v. Gray, 369 N.C. 1, 6–7, 789 S.E.2d 445, 448 (2016).

44. *Gray*, 369 N.C. at 7, 789 S.E.2d at 448–49 (distinguishing G.S. 1-50(a)(3)).

7.3 Railroad Crossings

The North Carolina General Statutes require railroads to construct tracks so "as not to impede the passage or transportation of persons or property" along streets.[45] North Carolina courts have long followed the majority rule that municipalities may require a railroad to construct or reconstruct, at its expense, grade improvements in streets in a manner that takes into account "the interest of public safety, convenience or welfare."[46] As the North Carolina Supreme Court explained, "The rationale of these cases is that the public has a superior right to the safe and unimpeded use of streets and highways and since the railroad has obstructed such use, the cost to the railroad is *damnum absque injuria* [(loss without injury)]."[47] In 1969, the court expressed concern about the constitutionality of requiring railroads to pay the entire expense of improvements that may benefit both the railroad and the public more generally, and suggested that the legislature was the appropriate branch of government to address the issue.[48] In response, the General Assembly enacted comprehensive legislation regulating the relationship between railroads and municipal streets and setting parameters for cost allocation.

G.S. 160A-298 reflects a general position that the primary purpose of a street is to move vehicular and pedestrian traffic. Thus, G.S. 160A-298 authorizes a municipality to "direct, control, and prohibit the laying of railroad tracks and switches in public streets and alleys and to require that all railroad tracks, crossings, and bridges be constructed so as not to interfere with drainage patterns or with the ordinary travel and use of the public streets and alleys."[49] A municipality may require installation of safety devices—such as signs, gates, and lights—at grade crossings and, if the governing body finds that a grade crossing "constitutes an unreasonable hazard to vehicular or pedestrian traffic," may require a grade separation.[50]

The statute directs that the costs of constructing, reconstructing, and improving street areas within areas covered by railroad cross ties, including the widening of these areas, is to be borne equally by the municipality and the railroad and that the costs of maintaining them is the railroad's exclusive responsibility.[51] The municipality may require warning and safety devices such as signs, gates, and lights, for which the municipality must pay 90 percent and the railroad 10 percent to install,

---

45. G.S. 136-192.

46. City of Raleigh v. Norfolk S. Ry. Co., 275 N.C. 454, 457, 168 S.E.2d 389, 391 (1969).

47. *Id.*

48. *Id.* at 459, 168 S.E.2d at 393.

49. G.S. 160A-298(a).

50. G.S. 160A-298(c).

51. G.S. 160A-298(b).

and the costs of maintaining such devices is to be split equally if installed after January 1, 1972.[52] There are different allocations for grade separations depending on the reason for the separation. If the municipality requires a separation with a bridge or overpass for an existing street, it must bear 90 percent of the cost and the railroad the other 10 percent.[53] The same allocation applies if a bridge must be changed due to street improvements.[54] The municipality must bear the full cost for a grade separation required for a new street and the railroad the full cost for a new track crossing an existing street.[55]

The North Carolina Secretary of Transportation has jurisdiction to require the elimination of grade crossings or placement of safety devices on grade crossings over streets and roads in the state system when in the interest of "public safety and convenience."[56] A state statute authorizes the Department of Transportation to allocate the cost according to the ratio of benefit to the railroad and to the public using the highway.[57] The department also is statutorily empowered to direct the raising or lowering of any tracks or roadway at any grade crossing in a municipal street that is not a link-in to or part of the state highway system, with the costs allocated by the Secretary of Transportation according to the same method as that applied to roads in the state system.[58]

---

52. G.S. 160A-298(c).
53. G.S. 160A-298(d).
54. G.S. 160A-298(e).
55. G.S. 160A-298(d).
56. G.S. 136-20, -20.1.
57. G.S. 136-20(b).
58. G.S. 136-195; 136-20(b).

Subject Index